Stressed
A Body M̶̶̶ ̶S̶p̶i̶r̶i̶t̶ ̶G̶u̶i̶d̶e̶ ̶t̶o̶
Creating a Happier and Healthier You
Volume 1

Dr. Jennifer Harrison

www.drjenniferharrison.com

Dear Lisa,
Wishing You All the Best!
Jen :)

COPYRIGHT

Dr. Jennifer Harrison, Stressed Self to Best Self™, PO Box 83062 14-11625 Elbow Drive SW, Calgary, AB, Canada, T2W 6G8 www.drjenniferharrison.com

ISBN 978-0-9947917-1-9

Cover photo Anna Dudko, Dreamstime.com. Cover design by Rob Williams at www.ilovemycover.com.

DEDICATION

I lovingly dedicate this book to the memory of my Mom and Dad who instilled in me the love of reading, life-long learning and the sharing of knowledge and experience to help others.

TABLE OF CONTENTS

ACKNOWLEDGEMENTS ix

INTRODUCTION xi

SECTION 1: BODYMIND HEALTH.. 1

CHAPTER 1: MEDITATION - WHICH TYPE IS RIGHT FOR YOU? 3

CHAPTER 2: DECREASE STRESS IN UNDER 90 SECONDS WITH THE CORTICES TECHNIQUE.................................... 9

CHAPTER 3: THE BASICS - BREATHING........................... 13

CHAPTER 4: THE BASICS - SLEEP 17

CHAPTER 5: NEW YEAR'S RESOLUTIONS VS GOAL SETTING 21

CHAPTER 6: A FRESH START.. 25

CHAPTER 7: 10 SECRETS TO KEEPING HEALTHY THIS WINTER.. 29

CHAPTER 8: HOW TO SHUT OFF YOUR MIND 35

CHAPTER 9: HOW TO SPRING CLEAN YOUR BRAIN...... 39

CHAPTER 10: A TIME FOR REBIRTH 43

CHAPTER 11: WHY FAILURE IS A GOOD THING 47

CHAPTER 12: YOUR HAPPY PLACE - MORE THAN JUST A CLICHÉ.. 51

CHAPTER 13: BACK TO SCHOOL, NOT BACK TO STRESS 55

CHAPTER 14: IS YOUR LAPTOP HURTING YOUR HEALTH?.. 59

CHAPTER 15: FIVE WAYS TO TURN A BAD DAY INTO A GREAT DAY 63

CHAPTER 16: ARE YOUR HABITS A HELP OR A HINDRANCE? 67

CHAPTER 17: SIX EASY SOLUTIONS TO SIX TIME WASTING PROBLEMS 71

CHAPTER 18: HOW TO AVOID THE TOP 5 TIME AND ENERGY WASTERS 73

CHAPTER 19: HOW TO BE A BETTER YOU 77

CHAPTER 20: AN ATTITUDE OF GRATITUDE - DOES IT MAKE A DIFFERENCE TO YOUR HEALTH? 79

CHAPTER 21: NOVEMBER IS PEACE MONTH 81

CHAPTER 22: HOW TO EXPERIENCE PEACE AND JOY THIS HOLIDAY SEASON 83

CHAPTER 23: 'TIS THE SEASON TO BE... 85

SECTION 2: NUTRITION 87

CHAPTER 24: THE BASICS - WATER 89

CHAPTER 25: THE SKINNY ON CARBS 95

CHAPTER 26: HEALTHY NUTRITION ON THE GO 99

CHAPTER 27: THE TOP FIVE SUMMERTIME FRUITS .. 101

CHAPTER 28: YOU ARE HOW YOU EAT 103

CHAPTER 29: WHERE, WHEN AND WHY YOU EAT MAY BE CAUSING YOU TO GAIN WEIGHT 107

CHAPTER 30: THREE TIPS FOR KEEPING OFF THE HOLIDAY POUNDS 113

SECTION 3: EXERCISE 115

CHAPTER 31: DAILY EXERCISE - HOW MUCH DO YOU REALLY NEED? 117

CHAPTER 32: JUNE IS NATIONAL ATHLETIC THERAPY MONTH.. 121

CHAPTER 33: GET FIT FOR FREE 123

CHAPTER 34: THE OLYMPICS - WHAT'S IN IT FOR US? 127

CHAPTER 35: HOW TO HAVE A SUMMER VACATION EVERY DAY.. 133

CHAPTER 36: SLIPPING INTO SEPTEMBER 137

CHAPTER 37: IS YOUR FITBIT HARMING YOUR HEALTH?.. 139

SECTION 4: RELATIONSHIPS.. 145

CHAPTER 38: HOW FALLING IN LOVE AFFECTS US RIGHT DOWN TO OUR DNA 147

CHAPTER 39: THE KEY TO A HEALTHY HEART - WHAT MOST DOCTORS DON'T KNOW 151

CHAPTER 40: WHO DO WE LOVE? 155

CHAPTER 41: GRIEF - THE FINAL FRONTIER.............. 159

SECTION 5: MONEY AND ABUNDANCE.......................... 167

CHAPTER 42: SO, YOU WANT TO WIN THE LOTTERY? 169

CHAPTER 43: HOW TO HAVE A STRESS FREE CHRISTMAS...WELL, ALMOST... 175

CHAPTER 44: CREDIT CARDS - FRIEND OR FOE?........ 179

CHAPTER 45: MONEY MATTERS 183

SECTION 6: THE BIGGER PICTURE 187

CHAPTER 46: CAN MEDITATION CREATE WORLD PEACE?.. 189

CHAPTER 47: CAN YOU BE ANGRY AND SPIRITUAL AT THE SAME TIME? 193

CHAPTER 48: CANCER - A FRESH PERSPECTIVE......... 197

CHAPTER 49: ANGELS - MYTH OR REALITY?................ 199

CHAPTER 50: IS THERE LIFE AFTER DEATH? 203

CHAPTER 51: THE POWER OF INTENTION - MORE THAN MEETS THE EYE 209

CONCLUSION: PUTTING IT ALL TOGETHER 215

ABOUT THE AUTHOR.. 217

ACKNOWLEDGEMENTS

I like to think of this section as my gratitude list. In addition to my Mom and Dad, to whom I dedicate this book, I have been incredibly blessed in my life by people who have loved, supported and challenged me along the way. In no specific order, I would like to express my deep appreciation for the following people:

I want to thank Jack Canfield, Steve Harrison, Stu McLaren, Peggy McColl, Jay Boyer and John Rhodes who, through sharing their knowledge and expertise, helped me get this book published.

Ana Caban is my favorite Pilates DVD instructor. In 2008, we had exchanged some emails and comments via her then web site, La Buena Life. Something she said combined with her positive outlook and encouragement helped to set me on the path that has (finally) resulted in getting my book completed!

Dr. Ron King was one of my clinical supervisors when I was at Chiropractic College. He is one of the few people I have ever considered to be a true mentor. One of the best gifts he gave me and other students was to teach us how to take both an intellectual and intuitive approach to treating patients. He is an amazing healer and I am blessed to also have him as my friend.

I'm very grateful for the profession of Athletic Therapy. I've had the pleasure to meet many Certified Athletic Therapists over the years who have been wonderful teachers, colleagues and students in my courses. All of them have enriched my life.

The BodyTalk System, which I started studying in 2001, has totally changed my life, both personally and professionally. I am grateful to Dr. John and Esther Veltheim for creating this amazing energy medicine health care and personal development system. I'm also grateful for everyone who is a part of the International BodyTalk Association and who continues to help with the evolution of BodyTalk.

I am blessed to work with an amazing group of people at Active Back to Health Centre. Also, my patients continue to inspire and amaze me.

My church has been, and continues to be, a wonderfully support-ive and nurturing community of faith. You truly are my spirit family and I am so grateful for all your prayers and the love and encouragement you have given me over the years.

The folks at WordPress Blogsites, particularly Kim DeJesus and Jody Luzier, have been amazing at helping me with my website as well as my book. Big thanks goes out to them. I also want to thank my editor Nicci Morris and cover designer Rob Williams.

I am very fortunate to have a multitude of dear friends and family members who have supported and encouraged me in various ways over the years. I am grateful for their love.

I am also grateful for all the teachers and students I've had along the way who have come in many different shapes, sizes and guises.

Well, as they say, "It takes a village" and so it does getting a book written and published!

INTRODUCTION

First of all, welcome and congratulations on choosing to Go From Your Stressed Self To Your Best Self™! If you are reading this book, it is probably because you are feeling overwhelmed with your life. I can appreciate how you may be feeling right now. Indeed, it was the fact that I was overwhelmed with my own life that actually inspired me to start writing a book as well as to create my membership website.

In May, 2009, I was really busy with working at the clinic, teaching courses, doing some volunteer work, plus my boyfriend at the time and I were having some major relationship issues and my home office was a disaster with books and papers piled up everywhere. I had just received an email from my favorite award-winning Pilates DVD instructor, Ana Caban. (For those of you not familiar with Caban, her Pilates DVDs have sold in the millions around the world and she's been featured in numerous magazines and on national talk shows.) I had been in email contact with Ana for a while and she offered to highlight me on her (then) new website, La Buena Life, if I had a book or something I wanted to feature. Instead of being elated at this offer, I felt overwhelmed! There I was, carrying my basket of dirty laundry to the laundry room saying to myself, "I have just received an amazing offer from Ana Caban and instead of being excited I'm stressed out! In fact, I am so overwhelmed I can't even bring myself to do anything with this great opportunity." I literally didn't know where to start. However, it was then doing laundry – you just never know when inspiration will hit you – that I had my "aha" moment and I knew I had to write a book about how to overcome being overwhelmed! Amazingly, at that moment, I also started to feel less stressed.

So, why has it taken me so long to publish this book? Well, like many of us, I worked on my book but continued to get sidetracked by life and my progress was much slower than I had planned on.

In 2013, I ended up creating my own membership website, literally from scratch. I had been writing and posting three new articles every month (which I continue to do) and while I love researching and writing the articles, it was taking time away from writing my book. However, it was at the end of 2014 that I had another inspiration and decided to compile the articles that I had already posted (which all follow the theme I had for my original book idea) and publish them as the book you are now reading. Some of the articles, which are now chapters, are seasonal or related to time specific events like the Sochi Olympics. However, they each contain helpful hints that can be applied at any time to help you live a happier and healthier life.

I have been very blessed in my life to have had some amazing teachers who have come in all shapes, sizes and disguises. I have also worked hard to use the tools I have learned to create health and happiness in my own life and to help others. A key observation from my clinical practice is that almost every new patient who comes to see me is stressed out. They have come seeking help because they don't know where to start and even making positive life changes seems daunting. There is no question that there are some amazing self-help/self-improvement books and courses available. Many of them have everything mapped out from A to Z and that is what some people are looking for. However, I know there have been times in my life when all that good advice felt more like a heavy weight than a life preserver. That is why I have created this first book in a series to help you start to make simple, doable but significant changes in six main areas of your life: Bodymind Health, Nutrition, Exercise, Money and Abundance, Relationships and something I call The Bigger Picture, which is a merging of science and spirituality. I've included resources at the end of each chapter, many of which are websites. At the time of publication, all resource links in the book were functional. To make it easier to access them, you may want to also purchase the eBook version of this book so you can simply click on the links.

Mark Twain is quoted as saying, "The secret of getting ahead is getting started. The secret of getting started is breaking your complex, overwhelming tasks into small manageable tasks, and then starting on the first one." Another saying I like is the famous Lao Tzu quote, "The journey of 1000 miles begins with one step."

I hope that reading this book will be a key step that will help you Go From Your Stressed Self To Your Best Self™!

SECTION 1: BODYMIND HEALTH

Dr. Jennifer Harrison

CHAPTER 1: MEDITATION - WHICH TYPE IS RIGHT FOR YOU?

Meditation, in its various forms, has been around for literally thousands of years. It can be found across many religions and cultures. Interestingly, in recent years, there has been a growing meditation movement in Western Culture and numerous research studies have been, and are continuing to be done, to answer the questions: Does meditation really work? (Yes!) How does meditation work?

In this chapter I want to briefly outline some different types of meditation, what some of the bodymind health benefits are, and provide you with a Progressive Relaxation Guided Meditation[1] that I created just for you! I'll also share some resources to help you decide which type of meditation is right for you.

When you meditate, physical changes actually happen in your body. Your brain waves change as do the activity in different parts of your nervous system. You transition from your "fight or flight" mode into your "rest and digest" or relaxation mode and your heart rate slows. There are many ways to meditate and many forms of relaxation contain aspects of meditation. The Mayo Clinic website lists different kinds of meditation.[2] Let's explore some types of meditation so you can see which ones may be right for you:

Guided Meditation: This involves using guided imagery or visualization in order to tune in to your body and mind to relax. You try to engage your five senses: sight, hearing, smell, taste and touch. Guided meditation usually involves you being led by a guide or teacher, either in a class or via an audio recording.

Mantra Meditation: This type involves repeating, either silently or aloud, a word or phrase (mantra) to draw attention away from distracting thoughts and bring total focus to the mantra. The mantra is co-ordinated with your breathing. An example would be, "As I breathe in relaxation, I breathe out tension."

Mindfulness Meditation: As the name suggests, this form of meditation is based on being mindful or expanding your conscious awareness to the present moment. The main focus is on your breathing. As thoughts and emotions pop into your mind, you observe them and release them, then return your focus to your breathing and the now. There is a great article in the Huffington Post[3] on the benefits of mindfulness meditation along with the research that is scientifically revealing how these benefits work. I've included a link to it in the Resources section.

Transcendental Meditation (TM): This form of meditation has its roots in the Vedic tradition of enlightenment from India. According to the Maharishi Mahesh Yogi, "The practice (of Transcendental Meditation) involves thinking of a word, a word devoid of meaning." These words or mantras usually involve sounds, such as "om", for example. The purpose of TM is to clear the mind and achieve a state of stillness of the mind.

Qigong: Qigong (sometimes spelled Qi gong) literally means "Life Energy Cultivation". It is pronounced CHEE-gung and it is a practice of aligning breath, movement, and awareness for exercise, healing, and meditation. Its roots are in Chinese medicine, martial arts and philosophy.

Tai Chi: Pronounced TIE-chee, this is a form of gentle Chinese martial arts. It involves performing a series of movements (each with a different name) in a slow, graceful manner while also focusing on deep breathing. When I was in my first year of Chiropractic College, a second year student, who happened to be a Tai Chi instructor, gave free classes every Wednesday at the end of the day. We were in classes 40 hours a week (not including studying) so by the end of each day, my brain was pretty much fried.

However, after only one hour of Tai Chi, I felt completely re-freshed. It was amazing!

Yoga: Yoga's origins are from India and there are many forms of yoga, not including the "North Americanized" versions that seem to keep popping up. In yoga you perform a series of poses and movements along with controlled breathing to promote a more flexible body and a calm mind. The practice of yoga allows you to focus on the present, on your body and breathing, thus shifting your focus away from the worries of the day.

I would like to add a few suggestions of my own:

Walking Meditation: A walking meditation can be done a few different ways. You can be outside or on your treadmill and with each step and/or each breath you can repeat a mantra such as "Peace" or "I embrace joy". You can use whatever mantra you want. You can also do a slower walking meditation, indoors or outdoors (although you may get some strange looks if you do this outdoors), where you take very slow, deliberate steps while using a mantra. Either way, continue to be mindful of your breath as well as your steps.

Using a Labyrinth: Labyrinths have an interesting history.[4] From prehistoric times to ancient Greek mythology, medieval Christian times to modern day movies, labyrinths have played a key role in the human journey. A labyrinth is a maze-like pattern that can take many forms from engravings on a piece of wood that you trace with your finger to large outdoor ones along which you can walk. In the past 20 years, there's been a resurgence of walking the labyrinth within various Christian traditions but many labyrinths are just intended to create mindfulness and to decrease stress. For example, several years ago an indoor labyrinth was created at the University of Calgary to help students decrease their stress during exam time. There is even a labyrinth locator website where you can search for labyrinths in your area or per-haps where you're planning to take your next vacation.[5]

Some research suggests that meditation may help the following conditions:

Allergies, anxiety disorders, asthma, binge eating, cancer, depres-sion, fatigue, heart disease, high blood pressure, pain, sleep dis-orders and substance abuse.

So, which meditation is right for you? Well, first off, most people say "I don't have time to meditate!" which, of course, is a sure-fire sign that you DO need to meditate. There is an old Zen saying that goes you should meditate for 20 minutes a day but if you are too busy, then you should meditate for an hour. Many people think that you have to set aside hours and hours to meditate. While you can certainly spend many hours meditating, you can achieve a meditative state within a few minutes, as you'll see when you do the Progressive Relaxation Guided Meditation that I created for you. The key with meditation, like with most things, is that in order to gain long lasting benefits from it, you need to create a meditation practice. In other words, you need to create a habit of meditating and getting into a meditative state daily.

If you go to the Transcendental Meditation web site[6] you'll see quotes from famous people like Paul McCartney, Ellen De-Generes, Hugh Jackman and others, stating how much TM helps them in their daily lives. Other leaders in the field of self-devel-opment such as Dr. Wayne Dyer and Jack Canfield all meditate as a daily part of their lives. Dr. Deepak Chopra promotes medi-tation and has great information on his web site[7]. Are these peo-ple super busy like we are? Absolutely! How are they able to do all the things they do in a day? In part, they meditate every day! I know from reading some of Dr. Wayne Dyer's books that he prac-ticed different types of meditation. I do, too, and I would encour-age you to do the same.

If you've never tried meditation before, I invite you to listen to the Progressive Relaxation Guided Meditation that I have created for you.[1] If you live in a larger centre, you can also check out local programs that teach meditation, tai chi, qigong, and/or yoga. Be sure to do some research on the instructor's credentials. If you live in a smaller center that doesn't offer any of these classes (although many of them do), again there are a lot of great DVDs, downloads and audio recordings available for you to try. Meditation opens up a whole new world and, more importantly, helps you Go From Your Stressed Self to Your Best Self™!

RESOURCES:

1. https://www.youtube.com/watch?v=YHhEAe79I1A
2. http://www.mayoclinic.com/health/meditation/HQ01070
3. http://www.huffingtonpost.com/2013/04/08/mindfulness-meditation-benefits-health_n_3016045.html
4. http://en.wikipedia.org/wiki/Labyrinth#Modern_labyrinths
5. http://labyrinthlocator.com/
6. http://www.tm.org/
7. http://www.chopra.com/ccl/sections/meditation

Dr. Jennifer Harrison

CHAPTER 2: DECREASE STRESS IN UNDER 90 SECONDS WITH THE CORTICES TECHNIQUE

Yes, there really is a simple yet powerful way to instantly decrease your stress in about 90 seconds! In fact, this technique not only decreases your stress but it also helps to enhance right and left brain communication and brain-body communication. It's easy to learn, easy to do and is totally safe for any one of any age. Sounding too good to be true? Well, it isn't. The technique is called the Cortices (CORT – uh – sees) Technique and it is one of the techniques of the BodyTalk System developed by Dr. John Veltheim. Cortices refers to the outer portion of the brain. However, the Cortices Technique is designed to actually help balance out all parts of the brain.

Next are three images to give you a visual of one of the most amazing organs in the body – the human brain! The first drawing is looking down on the top of the brain so you can see the two halves or hemispheres of the brain. The next is a drawing showing the lobes of the right half of the brain and the last image is an actual fMRI (functional magnetic resonance imaging) scan of the brain (the person is facing left) showing what the brain looks like when performing memory tasks. The white shaded areas are where there are higher levels of brain activity.

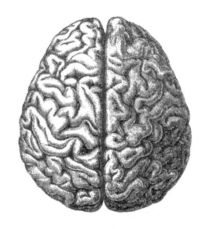

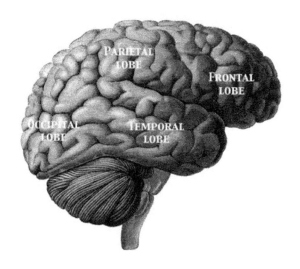

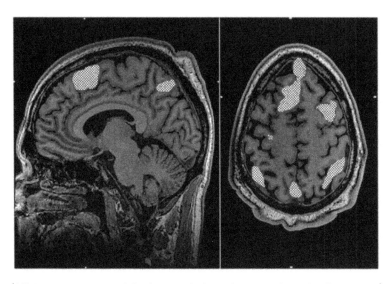

(All images are copyright free, including the second one by Camazine.)

The brain is divided into two halves – the right and left hemispheres as you saw on the first image. The two hemispheres are connected at the bottom so they can communicate with each other. When we get stressed, we get breakdowns in communication. Also, every disease or dysfunction occurring in the body is reflected in the brain, often resulting in an area with decreased blood flow which will show up as a "cold spot" on certain brain scans. Each hemisphere is further divided into lobes, shown in the second image. Here's a quick over view of the different lobes:

1. The FRONTAL lobes are at the front where your forehead is. The frontal lobes help you to learn, think and make decisions. It's also where the message comes from to move your muscles when you want to write an email, lift weights or go for a walk.

2. On the top of your brain are the PARIETAL lobes. This is where you receive sensation information from all of your body parts. It's also where you interpret taste information about what you are eating or drinking.

11

3. At the back of the brain are your OCCIPITAL lobes which translate information about what you see with your eyes.

4. Lastly, the lobes on the side of the brain are called the TEMPORAL lobes and that is where you receive and decipher information coming from your ears.

The brain does much more than this but I wanted to give you a general idea of some of the major functions.

I've prepared a video that will show you how to do the Cortices technique, or as we say in BodyTalk, *tap out your Cortices*. It's important to know that you can do the Cortices technique once a day or many times a day, depending on how stressed you are or how tired your brain is. I'll tap out my Cortices several times a day just to help re-charge my brain or to shift gears if I've had a busy day at work and want to relax to enjoy my evening. The technique is safe to do. If you happen to do the technique and your brain doesn't need balancing at that point in time, then simply nothing will happen, so you can do no harm. To watch the video, use the link below to go to my YouTube channel and look for the *Decrease Your Stress in Under 90 Seconds with The Cortices Technique* video.

https://www.youtube.com/channel/UCjW0ZDiq40-Pomu_iVbdhXw

I'd like to invite everyone to do a 30-DAY CORTICES CHALLENGE by tapping out your cortices at least once a day for the next 30 days. Keep track of your stress levels and see how they change over time.

CHAPTER 3: THE BASICS - BREATHING

Did you know that there is something that you do every day that has such a major impact in your life that it can literally be the difference between life and death? Did you know that even though you've been doing it since you were born, stress can make you do it incorrectly and cause huge health problems? If you haven't guessed yet what I'm talking about, it's breathing! In this chapter I'll show you how you can check to see if your breathing is causing health issues, and if so, how you can easily correct it, and much more!

Let's take a look at the following:

1. The health benefits of proper diaphragmatic breathing.

2. How you can check to see if you're breathing properly.

3. How you can correct your breathing when you're lying down and when you're sitting and standing.

4. How you can incorporate a simple breathing exercise that will help to decrease stress, improve your health and make you happier!

5. A free app you can download from either iTunes or Amazon (.ca or .com) that a patient of mine told me about.

On the one hand, everyone knows that if you stop breathing long enough, you die. However, I bet you didn't know that proper (diaphragmatic) breathing:

1. Helps your blood circulation, especially getting the blood flowing from your lower body back to the heart against gravity.

2. Helps get fuel (like sugar or glucose) and other nutrients to all the cells of your body, including the brain, heart, muscles, organs and skin.

Dr. Jennifer Harrison

3. Helps with lymphatic circulation which plays a key role in your immune system.

4. Helps massage your organs to aid in better food digestion.

5. Helps the liver to function properly. The liver works to get rid of toxins and store iron, among many other important things. It is actually attached to the underside of your diaphragm (breathing) muscle at the bottom of your rib cage and the liver needs you to breathe properly in order to do its job effectively.

6. Helps to support your lower back and therefore aids in all body movement.

7. Helps you to get in more oxygen and get rid of more carbon dioxide (a by-product of burning fuel/glucose).

8. Helps to decrease stress, stabilize moods, control anger and anxiety!

The majority of people do *not* breathe properly. So, in addition to negatively affecting all the things I listed above, improper breathing can also cause a lot of muscle problems in the neck and upper back leading to tight, painful muscles and joints in your spine, headaches and even cause you to become lightheaded.

Are you breathing properly? To check, sit comfortably and place one hand lightly over your upper chest and one hand over your abdomen. Now sit and breathe the way you usually do for about five breaths. Where do you feel the breathing happening? Is your chest moving more than your abdomen or is your abdomen moving more than your chest? If you're not sure, get a friend or family member to help you.

Now, lay down and do the same thing. When you're breathing the way you usually do, where do you feel it more, your chest or your abdomen?

If you get the chance to watch a baby breathe, they do it perfectly, all from the abdomen. This is called diaphragmatic breathing and it is the correct way to breathe when we're at rest. We all start out breathing this way, the proper way, but over time due to stress, societal pressure (as women and I'm sure some men, we tend to walk around with our tummies sucked in to look thinner) or health issues like asthma, we end up doing more upper chest breathing. We're usually not even aware of it and this creates an unhealthy pattern. Breathing is an interesting bodily function because, on the one hand, it's done automatically. We don't have to consciously tell ourselves to breathe all the time. Thank goodness, because we'd run into big problems when we fell asleep! On the other hand, we can control our breathing by tuning in to it and becoming consciously aware of how we are breathing. Yoga and Pilates, for example, place a large emphasis on tuning into and controlling breathing.

PLEASE NOTE: When you're exercising or doing vigorous physical activity, it is normal to breathe from *both* the abdomen and the chest. The chest expansion helps to bring in more oxygen and get rid of more carbon dioxide.

Well, now you know the wrong way to breathe and the health problems that can cause. What I'm going to show you now is how you can correct your breathing and decrease your stress with some very simple, brief exercises that you can easily incorporate into your day.

When you're learning to breathe properly again, it's easiest to do this when laying down on your back. I usually teach my patients to exaggerate pushing their abdominal muscles out as they breathe IN and exaggerate pulling their abdominal muscles in as they breathe OUT. You can continue to keep one hand resting lightly on your upper chest and one hand laying lightly on your abdomen. This will help you retrain your muscles. If you've been breathing improperly for a long time, this may feel very strange. It might even feel like it's the opposite of how it should be. However, this is the proper way to breathe. Repeat this exaggerated way of breathing 10 times.

I would recommend doing this every morning before you get out of bed and again before you go to sleep at night.

After doing this daily for one week, try the exercise in a seated position. You may find it more difficult, but just remember to exaggerate the abdominal muscle movement the same way you did lying down. The more you do it, the easier it will get. I would recommend doing this every hour throughout your day as well as the 10 breaths in and out before getting out of bed in the morning and going to sleep at night. After a week of this, then do the exercise when you're standing.

By incorporating these simple but powerful breathing exercises into your daily life, not only will you decrease your stress, but you'll be much happier and healthier!

RESOURCES:

1. The *Breathe2Relax* app is a great resource and easy to use. Plus, it's FREE!

For iPhone, iPod Touch or iPad: Go to the iTunes stores.

For Android devices: You can find it on Amazon.

CHAPTER 4: THE BASICS - SLEEP

There are three basics that I feel are essential to managing stress well: breathing properly, getting enough water (see "Chapter 24: The Basics - Water"), and sleep. An estimated 3.3 million Canadians age 15 years and older have problems getting enough sleep. This is affecting their health and quality of life. In addition to talking about the health risks of not getting enough sleep, I'm going to provide you with some hot tips on how to make sure you're sleeping the correct way! Yes, there are some definite dos and don'ts when it comes to sleeping habits. Some of them may come as quite a surprise!

While the general consensus is that there are many factors that affect the number of hours of sleep you need per night, the Center for Disease Control offers these general guidelines for various age groups[1]:

Newborns: 16-18 hours

Preschool-aged children: 11-12 hours

School-age children: at least 10 hours

Teens: 9-10 hours

Adults (including older adults): 7-8 hours

Pregnancy, aging, previous sleep deprivation and quality of sleep all play a role, too.

In a significant study done on sleep deprivation at the University of Chicago, researchers monitored a group of students who only got four hours sleep per night for six straight days. The volunteers developed higher blood pressure, higher levels of the stress hormone cortisol, produced only half the usual number of antibodies to a flu vaccine and also showed signs of insulin resistance, which

Dr. Jennifer Harrison

is a pre-cursor to Type 2 diabetes and metabolic slowdown.[2] Remember, this was only after six days of not getting enough sleep! This research helps explain why chronic sleep debt raises the risk of obesity, heart disease, stroke and diabetes.

The good news is that if you're not sleeping well, there are some straight forward action steps that you can take to help with that. The University of Maryland Sleep Disorders Center has some great suggestions to help you get a good night's sleep.[3] These involve your personal habits, sleeping environment, how you get ready for bed, where your TV is located and other factors. Let's take a look.

Your Personal Habits:

Fix a bedtime and an awakening time and stick to it.

Avoid napping during the day.

Avoid alcohol 4-6 hours before bedtime. While it may make you sleepy at first, a few hours later when your blood alcohol levels start to drop, there is a wake-up effect.

Avoid caffeine 4-6 hours before bedtime. Caffeine is a stimulant that excites your brain and entire nervous system and can also cause stomach upset and aggravate conditions like reflux (heartburn) which will prevent you from getting a good night's sleep.

Avoid heavy, spicy or sugary foods 4-6 hours before bedtime. Again, these types of food can also contribute to stomach or digestive system upset.

Exercise regularly, but not right before bedtime. Even though exercise is very good for you, it activates the same part of the nervous system that gets stimulated when we are stressed. That's why if you exercise right before bed time it can take even longer to fall asleep.

Your Sleeping Environment:

Use comfortable bedding. If the linens are not comfortable for your skin, that may prevent you from falling asleep easily. If the comforter is too heavy or you don't have enough blankets and are too cold, this will disrupt your sleep as well.

Find a comfortable temperature setting for sleeping and keep the room well ventilated.

Block out all distracting noise and eliminate as much light as possible. Some people find using a white noise generator helpful if they happen to live in a noisy neighbourhood. Also, blackout curtains can help to diminish light pollution.

Reserve your bed for sleep and sex. Don't use it as an office or workroom.

Getting ready for bed:

Try a light snack of warm milk or bananas (high in tryptophan) before bed to help you sleep.

Practice relaxation techniques before bed. Please refer to "Chapter 1: Meditation - Which type is right for you?" and "Chapter 2: Decrease Stress in Under 90 Seconds with the Cortices Technique". Don't take your worries to bed. This is a great opportunity to engage in your "Attitude of Gratitude" that I talk about in "Chapter 20: October is Attitude of Gratitude Month".

Establish a pre-sleep ritual:

Get into your favourite sleeping position, but don't sleep on your stomach as this is very hard on your neck. If you are a stomach sleeper, try sleeping on your side while you hug a pillow. It'll feel like you're sleeping on your stomach but will be much healthier for your neck and spine. I had to make this change a number of

Dr. Jennifer Harrison

years ago and since then, I've taught literally hundreds of my patients to do the same – with success!

TVs, laptops, tablets, cell phones and other electronic devices:

Watching TV, checking email, social media, etc. all excite the brain! You do NOT want to excite your brain before going to bed. You want to be relaxing your brain and your mind before bedtime. As mentioned before, your bed should be reserved for sleeping and sex. Leave all the electronics in your living room and home office/den.

I'll leave you with a word about sleep debt or trying to catch up on your sleep. Dr. Lawrence J. Epstein of the Harvard-affiliated Sleep Health Centers recommends the following:

"Settle short-term debt. If you missed 10 hours of sleep over the course of a week, add 3 or 4 extra sleep hours on the weekend and an extra hour or two per night the following week until you have repaid the debt fully.

Address a long-term sleep debt. Plan a vacation with a light schedule and few obligations. Then, turn off the alarm clock and just sleep every night until you awake naturally.

Avoid backsliding into a new debt cycle. Once you've determined how much sleep you really need, factor it into your daily schedule. Try to go to bed and get up at the same time every day – at the very least on weekdays."[2]

Sweet dreams!

RESOURCES:

1. http://www.cdc.gov/features/sleep/
2. http://www.health.harvard.edu/fhg/updates/Repaying-your-sleep-debt.shtml
3. http://ummidtown.org/programs/sleep/patients/sleep-hygiene

CHAPTER 5: NEW YEAR'S RESOLUTIONS VS GOAL SETTING

Happy New Year, Everyone! Whether you're nursing a hang-over, relieved to put the past year to rest or really excited about the upcoming year, this chapter is for you! Almost everyone makes New Year's Resolutions. According to Peggy McColl, NY Times Best Selling author, coach and mentor, here are some top 10 resolutions:

1. Spend more time with family and friends.

2. Get in shape.

3. Lose weight.

4. Quit smoking.

5. Enjoy life more.

6. Quit drinking.

7. Get out of debt.

8. Learn something new.

9. Help others.

10. Get organized.

Any of them look familiar? How many are on your list? According to a 2013 article by Forbes.com, only eight percent of people will achieve their New Year's Resolutions! Will you be part of that eight percent or will you be part of the 92 percent majority who fail to keep their resolutions? If you'd like to improve your chances of success, this chapter will help you do just that.

Resolutions are more like wishes or daydreams. We put them out there and hope for the best. They usually start out with great momentum and enthusiasm that quickly dwindle as we get back in the rut of our daily lives. Goals, on the other hand, are much different. Bestselling author and business man Harvey MacKay says that, "A goal is a dream with a plan and a deadline." For example, if you were to talk to any of the athletes getting ready to compete in the Olympics, how many of them do you think would say that they wrote down that they wanted to compete in the Olympics and then left it at that? Right, none of them would say that! Instead, they would tell you about all the smaller goals they set and the action plans that they created with help from parents, friends and coaches. They would go on to say how they devoted time and energy, both mentally and physically, toward achieving those smaller goals with the ultimate goal being competing or winning a medal at the Olympics.

So, you might be saying to yourself, "Well, that's fine, but how can I compete with Olympic athletes?" While you might not be hurtling yourself down a ski hill at 130 kph or sprinting in the 100 metre race, the basic approach that Olympic athletes use is the same approach that we can ALL use to achieve our goals. Here's how:

1. **Make a list** of what you would like to change or goals you would like to achieve for the year.

2. **Review the list** and pick your top three. Keep it simple.

3. Now, with each of these three goals, make another list of one or two things that you can do each day or each week that will help you achieve that goal. These are called **action steps**.

4. Review what you have written and ask yourself, **"Is this doable?"** For example, if one of your goals is to get into better shape and you're already working 45-50 hours per week and you're planning on going to the gym for a two hour workout six days a week, will you really have the time or energy to add another 12-14 hours a week to your schedule? Probably not. Or at least not

for long. However, what if you were to walk an extra couple of blocks to the next bus stop or take a couple of flights of stairs up to your office every day and then go the gym three days a week? Wouldn't this be more doable all the while still working toward your goal? *Chicken Soup for the Soul* best-selling author and success coach Jack Canfield talks about "chunking it down". What he means by this is to take a goal and then break it down into smaller, attainable goals. This is a sure-fire way to achieve success. That's why I suggested in step 2 to start by picking your top three goals out of your list, which may have 10, 20 or even 50 goals on it.

5. **Determine if your goal needs a deadline**. For example, if one of your goals is to get out of debt, figure out how much you're currently spending, how much money is actually coming in every month (refer to the Chapters in the Money and Abundance section of this book), and then set the amount of money you want to put toward your debts each month. Then set a date as to when you would like to see the debt paid off. The deadline may be six months. If it is a larger debt, then you may need to set a series of deadlines (chunking it down) so that you can mark your successes along your journey toward getting out of debt.

6. **Repetition.** Goals require that we create and reinforce new action steps or habits every day. For example, brushing your teeth daily may seem like a no brainer now, but when your parents were teaching you when you were young, what did they do? They showed you how to brush your teeth and for years repeatedly asked you each day, "Have you brushed your teeth?" Now it's a daily habit. Well, it's the same with achieving your goals. You have to reinforce that new action step or habit every day until you reach your goal.

7. **Cheer yourself on** and give yourself credit for all the little goals that you achieve en route to the bigger goal! If you have a rough week and get pulled off track (life happens to all of us), then just

Dr. Jennifer Harrison

go back to your plan that you wrote out for your top three goals and get back into the groove.

8. **Revisit your goals quarterly.** Every three months, check to see if you're on track or if you need to change any action steps or deadlines. If you're on a roll, you may even want to add another goal from your original list!

Remember, slow and steady wins the race! Here's to Your Best Self Year!

RESOURCES:

1. http://www.forbes.com/sites/dandiamond/2013/01/01/just-8-of-people-achieve-their-new-years-resolutions-heres-how-they-did-it/
2. Canfield, Jack, Switzer, Janet. *The Success Principles: How to Get from Where You Are to Where You Want to Be.* New York: HarperCollins, 2005.

CHAPTER 6: A FRESH START

While everyone else is talking about New Year's Resolutions, I want to talk about taking a different approach to the New Year. To me, New Year's Resolutions are nothing more than a wish list people create about things they want to change in their lives but have very little chance of actually accomplishing. "What is she talking about?" you say. I know. Sounds kind of harsh. However, statistics show that only 39 percent of people in their twenties actually achieve their New Year's Goals. For people over 50 it's an abysmal 14 percent![1] The problem is that resolutions with no action plan are just wishes that have very little chance of ever coming true. So as the gyms and yoga studios fill up every January with people wanting to lose weight and others plan on getting rich while trying to figure out how they will pay off their credit card bills from Christmas, what can you do so that this is your best year ever? If you really want to make some positive changes in your life, there are a series of steps you need to take in order to truly make a fresh start.

First of all, go ahead and make your "wish list" or New Year's Resolutions of all the things you'd like to change or achieve in your life. No matter how big or small, write down what you would like to accomplish in the upcoming year.

Next, pick your top three. Choose the three most important things you want to see happen in your life this year.

Now, I invite you to analyze these top three wishes using the S.M.A.R.T. system.[2] S.M.A.R.T. is an acronym that stands for:

• Specific
• Measureable
• Attainable
• Realistic
• Timely

Dr. Jennifer Harrison

For example, one of the consistent top 10 New Year's Resolutions that people make is to lose weight. If you were to look at losing weight using the S.M.A.R.T. system, the first thing you would need to do would be to get specific about the amount of weight you want to lose. Is it 5 lbs, 10 lbs, 50 lbs?

Next, how are you going to measure your success in losing weight? The most obvious answer is by stepping on the scales. However, did you know that muscle weighs more than fat? Did you know that sometimes when people start eating a healthy diet and exercise to build up muscle mass, they may, at some point actually start gaining weight? Initially, they may lose some pounds, but if they are consistent with weight training, they could conceivably gain pounds because of the increase in muscle mass. By saying you want to lose weight, essentially you are saying that you want to be healthier. So, what else are you going to measure? Waist and hip measurements? BMI (body mass index)? You need to be aware of the tools that will be accurate in helping measure your progress and ultimately, your success.

Is losing 50 lbs an attainable goal? Your medical doctor may have told you that because of your high blood pressure, diabetes or arthritic knees, you need to lose 50 lbs or more. How are you going to do that? What makes a goal unattainable? Well, for one, if it feels too intimidating, too "I'll never be able to do that" and you don't have a specific action plan in place, then you've set a goal that's probably unattainable. However, if you reframe it and decide to lose 5 lbs, followed by another 5 lbs and another until your reach your goal of 50 lbs (or whatever is the healthy goal), then you've made your "wish" an attainable target. You also need to be specific about how you're going to attain your goal. What dietary changes are you going to make? Are you going to exercise more? What exercises are right for you and how will you work them into your schedule? You need specific strategies that may involve working with a naturopathic doctor, nutritionist, athletic therapist, sport physiotherapist, chiropractor and perhaps a personal fitness trainer to help you make your goal not only attainable, but safe.

Following with this theme, the next thing to look at is if your weight loss goal is realistic. Perhaps you want to weigh 115 lbs like your favourite actress. If you're a guy, maybe you want to bulk up to look like your favourite action hero or professional athlete. With your height and bone frame, is it realistic for you to actually weigh 115 lbs or to bulk up to 215 lbs? More importantly, is that even a healthy weight for you? Also, how are you going to maintain that weight once you've achieved your goal? You may need to re-evaluate your "resolution" and choose something that is going to be more realistic for you.

The last thing to look at is whether your "wish" or "resolution" is timely. For example, if you want to lose 50 lbs in three months, is that a realistic time frame? Yes, there are some fad diets that could probably get you there in that amount of time. However, they are most likely unhealthy, perhaps even dangerous, and the probability of you maintaining your goal is very slim. What about looking at six, nine or 12 months? Is that a healthier and more realistic deadline to set for yourself?

Regardless of what your goals are, the other thing to remember about making a fresh start is that you're going to be working against existing habits that you've set over months, years or perhaps even a lifetime. One key to creating and maintaining new healthy habits is to be consistent. A way to help with that is to revisit your goals or resolutions at least every three months. Re-evaluate using the S.M.A.R.T. system. You may have to tweak a few things along the way or perhaps change the goal altogether. However, by re-visiting your goals regularly, you significantly increase your chances for success. Another key is to work on identifying some of your underlying belief systems that may have been preventing you from being successful in the past. There are a variety of techniques out there, including The BodyTalk System[3, 4], that can be helpful with addressing and changing these limiting belief systems.

I hope with the above examples you can see why, rather than making a list of New Year's Resolutions that have a low likelihood of success, I like to think of making a fresh start. Here's to Your Best Year Ever!

RESOURCES:

1. http://www.statisticbrain.com/new-years-resolution-statistics/
2. http://en.wikipedia.org/wiki/SMART_criteria
3. http://drjenniferharrison.com/bodytalk/
4. https://www.bodytalksystem.com/

CHAPTER 7: 10 SECRETS TO KEEPING HEALTHY THIS WINTER

With every news headline reporting flu outbreaks including the H1N1 virus, and even the Avian flu, everyone is on edge. The irony, of course, is that being afraid of getting the flu can actually contribute to stressing your immune system, thereby, increasing your chance of getting a cold or the flu! Don't get me wrong, no one wants to get the flu. Plus, the flu can be dangerous for people with compromised immune systems such as elderly people, those battling other diseases or people, including children, who are generally in poor health as a result of unhealthy nutrition and lifestyle habits.

However, I want to bring you a couple of pieces of good news! First of all, according to a January 3, 2014, article in the Huffington Post, Dr. Allison McGeer, head of infection control at Toronto's Mount Sinai Hospital and one of Canada's leading flu experts, is quoted as saying, "It'll be over in a month. There's been a fair amount of activity, but it's not terrible. And that should be it." She also goes on to say that different provinces report cases in varied ways which can give us misleading statistics. "Numbers don't mean much when it comes to seasonal flu and they probably shouldn't concern the public to any real degree, McGeer says."[1]

The second piece of good news is that while the news headlines continue to focus on the negative, I want to share with you 10 secrets that can help keep you and your family healthy during the winter cold and flu season! I haven't had a full-blown cold in almost three years (and prior to that it had also been three years). The last time I had the flu was over 10 years ago and it only lasted a few days. How is that possible? Read on to find out how as I share my health secrets with you!

I want to share something else with you. I was really sick when I was a kid. I almost died from a respiratory infection when I was

29

six weeks old, I had pneumonia and whooping cough when I was two years old and I had repeated respiratory infections all through my childhood. When I was six, I was finally diagnosed with asthma and allergies to cigarette smoke, fur, feathers and house dust. While I outgrew the asthma and most of my allergies, as an adult, I would still get at least three or four major colds a year, sometimes even bronchitis. However, since 2002 I've gotten full blown colds, on average, once every three years or so! I'll get a mild sore throat or sniffles here and there, but they never last more than two or three days. How is this possible? Well, here are my 10 secrets to keeping healthy, not only through the winter, but all year round.

1. Drink lots of water. We lose about 2 litres of fluids every day through breathing, sweating, urinating and defecating. According to the Mayo Clinic, The Institute of Medicine determined that an adequate intake (AI) for men is roughly 3 litres (about 13 cups) of total beverages a day. The AI for women is 2.2 litres (about 9 cups) of total beverages a day. While we can obtain some fluids through our food (especially from food such as watermelon and tomatoes), we need to get fluid from other sources. Now, they go on to say that juice and milk count as fluids. However, they recommend that the bulk of your fluid intake should be water because it's calorie-free, inexpensive and readily available.[2]

2. Eat nutritious foods. Getting a balance of fruits, veggies and protein in each meal and in snacks goes a long way to keeping your immune system strong. Excess refined sugars found in donuts, candies, soda pop and desserts can actually lower your immune system.

3. Get regular exercise. Exercise is a great way to decrease stress which also helps your immune system to be healthy. It doesn't have to be anything overly vigorous. Just going for a walk, doing yoga or Pilates can be very beneficial.

4. Get some sleep! This is one of the most important things that you can do to not only decrease stress, but get and stay healthy. Burning the candle at both ends is a sure-fire way to get sick. It's also the reason why so many people who do get colds or the flu, stay sick much longer than they should.

5. De-stress. Chronic high or even low grade stress has been shown to lower your immune system and make you more susceptible to getting sick. In order to de-stress you have to get out of "fight or flight" mode and into "rest and repair" mode. In order to do that, you must intentionally do something to make that happen. Activities such as meditation, yoga, tai chi, qi gong and even breathing exercises can help you to relax. By clearing your mind of the daily clutter and just focusing on "the now", you help your body get into rest and repair mode which is good for your immune system and the rest of your bodymind.

6. Do things that make you happy. Spending fun times with family and friends or just spending time doing something, like a hobby, that makes you smile is a great way to decrease stress. Decreased stress means a happier, healthier immune system.

7. BodyTalk. I first started studying BodyTalk in 2001 and it has changed my life and health in so many ways that I can't imagine it not being an integral part of my life! BodyTalk is a consciousness based energy medicine technique which is part of the larger BodyTalk System. The main focus of BodyTalk is to re-establish communication links within the body and mind that have become broken due to stress, injuries and illnesses. It also takes into account that our belief systems play a huge role in our bodymind health. Remember when I told you earlier how sick I used to get all the time? Well, that all changed once I became a Certified BodyTalk Practitioner and began receiving regular BodyTalk sessions. I also do BodyTalk on myself every day, including doing BodyTalk Access which I'll talk about next. (Please see number 3 in the Resources section for a link to my YouTube channel where there is a video called *What is BodyTalk?*)

8. BodyTalk Access. BodyTalk Access was created in 2005 and I became an Access instructor in 2007. BodyTalk Access is a one day course for lay people where you learn five of the basic BodyTalk techniques that make up the BodyTalk Access routine. The Access routine only takes about 10 – 15 minutes to do. I do this once a day, more often if I feel like I'm fighting off a cold. It helps to decrease stress, allow your body to utilize water more effectively, boost your immune system and help your muscles and joints to work effectively, all while helping to balance out your body's energy systems. For more information, check out my YouTube channel for a video I did about BodyTalk Access for the International BodyTalk Association in 2011.[3] (Please see the Resources section.)

9. Reiki. I first studied Reiki in 1999 and to date, I have completed my level II Reiki training. Although I'm not allowed to use it as part of my chiropractic practice, I use it regularly on myself (as well as with friends when they request it). We are energy beings and there's a continuing growing body of research that supports this. When there are energy disruptions due to stress, this can lead to injuries and illnesses. We often think that the injury or the illness caused the mental and emotional stress but the research suggests that it is actually the other way around. Reiki is being used in many hospitals in North America and there is some interesting research being done showing the benefits such as boosting the immune system.[4] I use Reiki to balance my energy, calm my mind and to address any bodymind health concerns I may have. I find that although Reiki is a very different technique from BodyTalk, it ties in very nicely with it.

10. Try to surround yourself with positive things. A number of years ago I realized that watching the news every day made me frustrated and stressed, as did watching mindless shows on TV, just for something to do. So, I decided to only read books that were positive and uplifting. I chose to watch movies and TV shows that made me feel good. I stopped watching the news and chose, instead, to listen to a news radio station for a few minutes on my way to work to catch the main headlines and keep current. I also became more aware of how many "Ain't it awful!" conversations I had with people and tried to engage in more positive conversations whether they be with my patients or family and friends. Jack Canfield talks about staying away from the "Ain't it awful" club and to spend more time with people who are positive and working on making positive changes in their lives. Now this doesn't mean that I don't go on a rant from time to time and vent to my friends. We all go through challenging times in our lives when we're sad, worried or upset. There's nothing wrong with experiencing these human emotions. We're programmed to have them. The problem arises when you get stuck in an emotion like sadness or anger. However, by focusing more on being positive and surrounding yourself with uplifting books, music, movies, TV shows and conversations, it helps you to be both happier and healthier!

I hope these 10 secrets for staying healthy this winter will be as helpful to you and they have been and continue to be for me! Here's To Your Best Self!

RESOURCES:

1. http://www.huffingtonpost.ca/2014/01/03/h1n1-canada-alberta-deaths-flu_n_4538628.html
2. http://www.mayoclinic.org/healthy-lifestyle/nutrition-and-healthy-eating/in-depth/water/art-20044256
3. https://www.youtube.com/channel/UCjW0ZDiq40-Pomu_iVbdhXw
4. Reiki and the immune system:
http://www.ncbi.nlm.nih.gov/pubmed/22132706

Dr. Jennifer Harrison

CHAPTER 8: HOW TO SHUT OFF YOUR MIND

How many thoughts do you have in a day, an hour, a minute? How many of these thoughts are repetitive? How many thoughts are positive? How many are negative? Does your mind keep working overtime even when your day is done and you're trying to fall asleep? Does your mind wake you up in the middle of the night endlessly looping negative or worry-some thoughts? In Buddhism, this agitated, constant mind chatter is referred to as "monkey mind". The Buddha is quoted as saying, "Just as a monkey swinging through the trees grabs one branch and lets it go, only to seize another, so too, that which is called thought, mind or consciousness arises and disappears continually both day and night."[1] In this article I'm going to share with you three simple methods that you can use to quiet this "monkey mind" to help you shift and Go From Your Stressed Self To Your Best Self™!

Many of you have heard me talk about the Cortices Technique, a simple yet powerful technique that comes from the BodyTalk System. I have been doing BodyTalk since 2001 and the Cortices Technique is still my "go to" when I have had a busy day or am going through a stressful time. The technique, which we often just refer to as "tapping out your Cortices", involves various hand positions over the brain, light tapping over your head and heart, as well as deep breathing. The purpose of tapping out your Cortices is to enhance right and left brain communication, brain-body communication as well as to decrease stress. We tap over the head to help stimulate the brain to re-establish communication links that have been broken due to injury, illness or stress. We tap over the heart to commit to the body's memory that we have re-established these communication links. Research shows that the electromagnetic field of the heart, which can be measured up to and beyond 15 feet away from the body, stores information about what's happening in the body. (Please see Chapter 2 to learn how to do the Cortices Technique).

Dr. Jennifer Harrison

In his wonderful book, *The Wise Heart: A Guide to the Universal Teachings of Buddhist Psychology*, Jack Kornfield, PhD, talks about the "storytelling mind."[2] This is similar to the monkey-mind concept I talked about earlier. The storytelling mind refers not only to rapidly changing busy thoughts, it also includes the scenarios we create and play over and over in our minds. Sometimes the stories are a re-telling of something that has actually happened to us. Sometimes it's an edited version of events, how we wish things had actually occurred. Often, it's scenarios we create that are focused on the "what ifs". "What if I get really sick and can't work? What if I lose all my savings? What if my husband/wife/partner leaves me? What if I never meet 'the one'?" It can often be our judgemental or critical mind. "I'll never be successful. I'll never be good enough. I'm not lovable."

Buddha is quoted as saying, "Who is your enemy? Mind is your enemy. Who is your friend? Mind is your friend. Learn the ways of the mind. Tend the mind with care."[2] Very few, if any of us, are taught as children ways to "tend the mind". These days it's all about movies and video games. I've had numerous patients tell me they plop their children down in front of the TV or computer so they'll stay still while they are eating a meal. I've had patients note that their children were having trouble with free play. What they meant was that their kids had become so accustom to structured play (activities that were already planned out for them) that they were at loose ends when given the opportunity to use their own imagination or to choose which games they'd like to play. Because most of us in the Western world aren't taught mind quieting skills as children, we often don't learn these techniques until we're adults, usually as a result of extreme stress or a crisis.

Dr. Kornfield recommends an exercise that helps to start bringing awareness to the repetitive thoughts or stories we create and re-tell in our minds throughout the day. He suggests that we write down our "top ten tunes" and name them. This is a form of mind-fulness. The more aware we are of how our minds are hindering us, the more we can take actions steps to "tend" our minds so that they are helping us. So, what are your top ten tunes of repetitive thoughts or scenarios that replay in your mind throughout the day and sometimes night? Once you've written them down, you can start changing them and replacing them with positive more empowering thoughts.

Another simple but powerful way to quiet your mind is to use a mantra. A mantra is a word, phrase or sound that helps us to con-centrate and clear our minds. Mantras are combined with deep breathing and are simple but powerful tools that can not only help us quiet our minds, but also create and maintain our focus and, of course, decrease stress. A couple of my favourite mantras are "I breathe in relaxation, I breathe out tension." This is co-ordi-nated with relaxed deep inhalations and exhalations. Another one is just to focus on the word "Peace" with each breath in and out. You can also use the Christian Scripture Psalm 46:10, "Be still and know that I am God", again combined with deep, peaceful breathing. The well-known sacred mantra, "Om", has Hindi ori-gins but is used across many religions including Hinduism, Bud-dhism and Sikhism. It is associated with various symbols, as well. Hindus believe that "as creation began, the divine, all-encompass-ing consciousness took the form of the first and original vibration manifesting as the sound 'OM'."[3] Whatever mantra you choose, know that this is a powerful way to quiet and clear your mind, restore and maintain a healthy focus and rejuvenate your body.

I hope you find these three mind clearing methods useful. They are great ways to help you Go From Your Stressed Self To Your Best Self™!

RESOURCES:

1. http://www.buddhisma2z.com/content.php?id=274

Dr. Jennifer Harrison

2. Kornfield, Jack. *The Wise Heart: A Guide to the Universal Teachings of Buddhist Psychology.* New York: Bantam Books, 2008. pp. 137,142.
3. http://en.wikipedia.org/wiki/Om

CHAPTER 9: HOW TO SPRING CLEAN YOUR BRAIN

Well, it's March and soon officially it will be spring, even if we keep having weather that makes us think that spring will never come. Soon, we'll also be thinking about spring cleaning – getting rid of clutter that has built up over the winter months, washing floors and windows and dusting the little nooks and crannies that we never seem to get to. However, have you thought about *spring cleaning your brain*? I don't know about you, but my brain can definitely get cluttered with the busyness of day to day life, let alone planning for future events and just trying to get everything done on my "to do" list. Sound familiar? Well, I have some easy, yet really effective techniques to share with you that you can use to not only spring clean your brain, but keep it clutter free year round!

1. The Cortices Technique: This is a technique that is part of the BodyTalk System. It's an energy medicine technique that anyone can learn how do to, and it takes less than 90 seconds to do. The purpose of the technique is to enhance left and right brain communication, brain-body communication as well as to decrease stress. (To learn this technique, please refer back to Chapter 2.)

2. Drink water: When your brain is fully hydrated it is approximately 80 percent water. Your brain needs water to function properly and when we're under stress, this is even more critical. How much water should you drink? Well, the average person loses about 2 – 3 L of water per day through urination, defecation, perspiration and even the moisture in their breath. The Mayo Clinic recommends men to have a fluid intake of approximately 3 L and women 2.2 L.[1] Remember that some of our food counts toward fluid intake. Factors affecting our need for water include climate (we sweat more when it's hot out), physical activity (we sweat more when we exercise), illness (it's easy to become dehydrated from vomiting and diarrhea when we're sick), diet (caffeine and alcohol act as diuretics and cause us to lose water) and stress. So the next time you're thinking of grabbing another cup of coffee or a diet soda, grab a glass of water instead! Your brain *and* body will love you for it.

3. Write it down: When your mind is cluttered, a great way to clear it is to write things down. Whether it is a grocery list, a daily or weekly "to do" list or active journaling, this really helps to clear your mind. Journaling can be especially effective if we're going through a difficult time or trying to come up with solutions to problems we're dealing with. Of course with technology you can also type it or dictate it! Lots of options. The key thing is to get it out of your brain so your mind can relax a bit. When I have a lot of things on my plate, I'll often write everything down and then review the list to prioritize what really needs to be done that day and what can wait for later.

4. Sleep: This is the wonderful magical time when our mind and body are supposed to rest and rejuvenate. However, most people are sleep deprived. The brain absolutely needs rest. Did you know that sleep deprivation has been used as a means of torture and brain washing? What's worse is that most of us do it to ourselves by not getting enough sleep! And, it's not just the hours of sleep but also the quality. Most people are watching TV, checking email or Facebook right up until bedtime. Research shows that this type of stimulation just before bedtime is not good for the brain.[2] Try tapping out your Cortices to relax your brain before going to bed. Even listening to a quiet guided meditation before bedtime will help you sleep better.

Well, here's to Spring Time and Spring Cleaning!

RESOURCES:

1. http://www.mayoclinic.org/water/ART-20044256

2. http://umm.edu/programs/sleep/patients/sleep-hygiene
3. http://ummidtown.org/programs/sleep/patients/sleep-hygiene

Dr. Jennifer Harrison

CHAPTER 10: A TIME FOR REBIRTH

Whether Easter is an important Christian holiday for you, a time to hunt Easter eggs or simply a sign of spring, it *is* a time of resurrection and rebirth. What do I mean by that? Well, after a long, cold winter we're longing for new grass and flowers to start growing, maybe even longing for some changes to happen in our bodies and minds after becoming stuck in a rut through the winter. A major sign of stress is when we get in a rut with daily routines or habits and repetitive thoughts that drain us and drag us down. So, how do you infuse some springtime newness into your life and decrease stress? How can you experience a rebirth?

Before you can move forward, you need to take stock of where you are right now. What things are you tired of in your personal life, family life and your work life?

1. Pick one thing you'd like to change in each area of your life. This may be something large like actually getting a new job or getting out of your current relationship if it's not healthy for you. It could also be something small like maybe rearranging the furniture in your living room, doing something fun with your family once a week like having a games night or going out to the park.

2. Review what things bring you joy. I asked this of one of my patients recently and they weren't able to give me an immediate answer. It was definitely time for them to re-evaluate and cultivate joy in their life! It might be something big like planning a trip or vacation. It might be something small like listening to music on your drive to work instead of the news on the radio. Focus on doing something once a day that brings you joy.

3. Try something new! Often when we get in a rut, we lose energy to even try new things. However, with a little effort, we can start making some changes that will bring newness and rebirth into our lives. Something simple like trying out a new recipe can shift things around. Driving home taking a different route each day or

43

adding an accessory like a scarf or tie that we don't usually wear can go a long way to lifting our spirits. Exercise, even something easy like going for a walk, can help get rid of stagnant energy. In Chinese medicine, the Wood element is associated with spring-time and newness, a shift in qi or body energy. I decided to do a 25 minute qigong workout recently that I have on one of my fitness DVDs. I hadn't done it in months and I couldn't believe how much better I felt![1]

4. Make small changes daily. I find it interesting that as human beings, we're always looking for something new – the latest movie, electronic device or the hottest new look in fashion. However, at the same time, we are creatures of habit to the point of stagnation. We get up at the same time every morning, have the same breakfast every day, we take the same route to work, wear the same outfits and watch the same TV shows over and over again every week. So how do we find a way to experience a rebirth or to resurrect our lives? Many times it's making little changes each day that produce the most profound results. Deciding to eat something different each day for breakfast, tapping out your Cortices (refer to "Chapter 2: Decrease Stress in Under 90 Seconds with The Cortices Technique") at the start and end of each day, choosing to read a new book each month to further your personal/spiritual growth – you'll be amazed at how just doing these few things will lead to a newness in your life, simple changes that can lead to a rebirth!

RESOURCES:

1. Gaiam *5 Day Fit Chi* DVD. It has 3 Tai Chi and 2 Qigong workouts on it. It's very gentle on the body but a powerful way to shift the energy in your bodymind. (Please note that I am not affiliated with Gaiam in any way. I personally own this DVD and have found it to be very helpful so I wanted to share that information with you.)

Dr. Jennifer Harrison

CHAPTER 11: WHY FAILURE IS A GOOD THING

What do the Wright Brothers, the creators of the *Chicken Soup for the Soul* books and Ellen DeGeneres have in common? They all experienced failure on a grand scale before they achieved success. Not only that, it was their failures that played a key role in helping them be successful in their respective fields. Let's take a closer look at why failure is a good thing.

Before the Wright Brothers invented the airplane in 1903, they actually studied all the failures of other inventors who had gone before them.[1] There were other flying machine designs that came out before Wilbur and Orville created theirs. However, they had all failed, in many cases resulting in the death of the person who decided to test fly their own designs! Even the Wright brothers crashed the first two gliders they designed in 1900 and 1901. However, they persevered, learned from the failures of others as well as their own. Thanks to that, today we can now book a flight to literally anywhere in the world – even a select few get to go to the International Space Station!

Another example of failure leading to success involves Jack Canfield and Mark Victor Hansen who are the creators of the *Chicken Soup for the Soul* books.[2] These inspirational books have sold over 500 million copies in over 100 countries around the world. However, it wasn't an overnight success story for them. Jack and Mark pitched their first book to over 140 publishers before they met a publisher who was willing to take a chance on them. That means that they received over 140 rejection letters before their books took off! Even best-selling mystery writer Agatha Christie received rejections for five years before she sold her first book. Now her books sales have exceeded $2 billion!

Yet another example is the famous comedienne and talk show host Ellen Degeneres.[3] After graduating from high school, she went to University but ended up dropping out after the first semester. While she did have a lot of success as a stand-up comedienne as well as a successful sit com called *Ellen* from 1994-1998, a follow up TV show in 2001 called *The Ellen Show* got terrible ratings and was cancelled after just one season. However, she didn't let her failures stand in her way. In 2003, she launched her day time talk show which continues to be wildly successful and also inspires kindness and generosity.

Imagine how different our lives would be if these and countless others had decided to give up after experiencing failure!

What failures have you had in your life? Have you ever failed a test? Had a failed marriage or relationship? Have you ever been fired from a job because you failed to meet certain quotas or expectations?

Over the years, my perception of "failure" has changed. We're taught at an early age that failing is a bad thing. But what if we looked at it differently? What if we reframed the concept of failure? What if we looked at our so-called failures as valuable life lessons instead?

When I look at some of my past relationships, instead of looking at them as failures and a complete waste of time and emotional energy, I've come to appreciate them for the valuable life lessons they taught me regarding self-respect and needing to honour and love myself more.

In my opinion, the only way you can really fail is if you don't learn anything from your mistakes, or if you don't even try in the first place. So, I invite you to revisit some of your so-called failures and look at them in a new light. What did you learn from them? How did they make you a better person? How were you able to take what learned to help others?

I love the saying, "What would you attempt to do if you knew you could not fail?" Looking at "failures" in a new way is great way to Go From Your Stressed Self To Your Best Self™!

RESOURCES:

1. http://www.wrightbrothers.org/History_Wing/Wright_Story/Wright_Story_Intro/Wright_Story_Intro.htm
2. http://www.literaryrejections.com/best-sellers-initially-rejected/
3. http://www.imdb.com/name/nm0001122/bio?ref_=nm_ov_bio_sm

Dr. Jennifer Harrison

CHAPTER 12: YOUR HAPPY PLACE - MORE THAN JUST A CLICHÉ

How many times have you made fun of needing to go to your "happy place" while recounting a crazy situation you've experienced? At one time or another we've all joked or been teased about going to our happy place to deal with stress. We've heard it on sitcoms and in movies to the point where "your happy place" has become a cliché. However, what you may not know is that research has been and continues to be done on happiness and the important effects happiness has on everything from personal health to the world economy. This chapter will help show you how to go to your happy place and reap the benefits.

In 2012, the first ever World Happiness Report commissioned for the United Nations Conference on Happiness was presented.[1] The results were quite interesting. Denmark, Norway, Finland and The Netherlands were rated as the happiest countries in the world whereas the least happy countries were found in Africa - Togo, Benin, Central African Republic and Sierra Leone. However, the worldwide report suggested that there are common denominators that help determine happiness.

While happier countries tend to be richer countries, there actually are more important factors linked to determining happiness, such as:

1. Social factors like the strength of social support, the absence of corruption and the degree of personal freedom.

2. Over time as living standards have risen, happiness has increased in some countries, but not in others (like the United States, for example).

3. Unemployment causes as much unhappiness as bereavement or separation. At work, job security and good relationships do more for job satisfaction than high pay and convenient hours.

4. Behaving well makes people happier.

5. Mental health is the biggest single factor affecting happiness in any country. Yet only a quarter of mentally ill people get treatment for their condition in advanced countries and fewer in poorer countries.

6. Stable family life and enduring marriages are important for the happiness of parents and children.

7. In advanced countries, women are happier than men, while the position is mixed in poorer countries.

8. Happiness is lowest during middle age.

So what are we supposed to do with this information to help us experience more happiness in our own lives? Some research published in March, 2008, in the journal Psychological Science suggested our personality traits which predispose us to happiness have a strong genetic component. However, the study also suggested that "around 50 per cent of the differences between people in their life happiness is still down to external factors such as relationships, health and careers."[2] What this means is that we have opportunities to create our own happiness and to create resiliency in the face of life's challenges.

Let's look at relationships. If you haven't found your "soul mate" yet, that doesn't mean that you can't have other significant positive relationships in your life. Friendships, family and other social connections are very important to your bodymind health. I like the advice that Jack Canfield and Janet Switzer give in their book *The Success Principles: How to Get From Where You Are to Where You Want To Be.*[2] They say don't join the "Ain't it awful" club or if you do belong, get out! What they mean by this is if the people you're hanging around with tend to only focus on the negative, start meeting and spending time with people who focus more on the positive. This also means shifting your own perspective if you tend to be always complaining about your life or things in general.

What about your health? While genetics do play a role, research is showing that it's a much smaller role than we think. Our belief systems, the action steps we take each day to deal with stress and to create positive situations in our lives actually have a powerful impact not only on our health, but also on our genes! Our body physiology literally changes when we're happy.[3] Plus, things like eating a healthy diet, getting regular exercise and getting adequate sleep go a long way in attaining and maintaining good health. If you have an existing health issue, get the professional health care you need to deal with it.

What about careers? Whether you're a stay at home mom, a plumber, a teacher or the head of a huge charitable organization, the most important thing is to love (or at the very least like) what you do and the people with whom you work. Many folks tend to paint themselves into a corner with regard to careers. They think that the highest paying job is the way to go or that they need to follow in the footsteps of their parents or follow other's expectations. However, you really have to follow your heart! If what you love to do doesn't pay the bills, at least try to have a job doing something that you enjoy with people who also enjoy their work. Then, create time to do what you love to do, which may include volunteer work.

OK, so even if you have great relationships, are healthy and have a great career, there are going to be times in life when you're faced with big challenges like the illness or death of a loved one, the downsizing of your workplace or some other unexpected stress event. It's at times like this that we need to go to "our happy place" and one way to do this is to write down memories of times or places when you were really happy. If you have photographs, even better. Keep this handy so that when you are hit with either low

Dr. Jennifer Harrison

grade ongoing stress or a high stress event, you can focus on your happy place and really feel the joy. Going to your happy place is more than a cliché. It's imperative for your health and well-being!

RESOURCES:

1. http://www.happinessresearchinstitute.com/world-happiness-report-release/4578771599
2. Canfield, Jack and Switzer, Janet. *The Success Principles: How to Get From Where You Are to Where You Want to Be.* New York: HarperCollins, 2005.
3. http://psychcentral.com/news/2008/03/05/genetic-link-to-happiness/2003.html

CHAPTER 13: BACK TO SCHOOL, NOT BACK TO STRESS

Isn't is appalling? Just as you're getting your summertime groove on, all of a sudden there are "End of Summer Sales" popping up everywhere and the dreaded "Back to School Sales". Whether you're going back to school, you have kids who are going back to school or even if you don't fall into either of these categories, the Back to School stress is palpable. I see it in my practice every year immediately after Labour Day Weekend, sometimes even in the last week of August. Everyone gets super busy and their stress levels go way up! However, it doesn't have to be this way. You actually can enjoy the rest of the summer and be ready for the back to school rush. That's right – you can still enjoy your back-yard BBQ bliss and be ready to slide into the post Labour Day busyness. Here's how.

FIVE HOT TIPS TO DECREASE STRESS:

1. If you have kids going back to school, go to your local dollar store to get the bulk of your children's schools supplies. You can save a bundle by purchasing the basics like loose leaf, pencils, pens, erasers, crayons, etc. at these discount stores. That means that you will have extra money to splurge on a few of the "must have" items that kids want like the latest action hero or Hello Kitty back pack. Get this done as soon as you can to avoid the stressful last minute rush.

2. The same goes for kids' back to school clothes. Get the basics at discount or consignment stores and that will give you more money to splurge one or two special outfits for the kids. Again, get this done early in August to avoid the rush.

3. Take 30 minutes to create meal plans for the first week back at school. By taking just a bit of time to plan ahead (you can actually do this while lounging in your back yard) you can make that first

week in September a whole lot easier. I'm a huge fan of slow cookers. (In the Resources section, I give you the names of some of my favourite recipe books that have made my life so much easier.) By choosing a few of your favourite healthy recipes, you can not only easily create your grocery list, but you can also prepare some great, nutritious meals ahead of time and save them in your freezer until you need them. Also, by planning nutritious lunches for the kids ahead of time, it'll make it less stressful for you *and* for your kids. Keep the grocery list handy like on your fridge or your smart phone. Whether you have school age kids or not, this is a strategy I use all the time. I prepare a slow cooker meal at the start of the week, keep a few servings in the fridge and freeze the leftovers. By doing this each week, I build up a nice variety in my freezer and this helps to ensure that I'm getting nutritious, yummy meals that I wouldn't have the time or energy to prepare each night during the week. Good nutrition is essential all the time, but it's even more important when we're under stress, like transitioning into the post Labour Day busyness.

4. A week before school starts, get back into your regular bed time and waking time routine. This is especially important for kids and teenagers who usually get into the summer vacation mode of staying up late and sleeping in late. Although you'll get some resistance from your kids, in the long run it'll be less stressful on everyone if you do this. Plus, it will also be healthier for everyone. Even if you don't have kids, this is a smart strategy to use.

5. Once you've taken a bit of time to plan and act ahead (it will really only take you several hours to create benefits that will last at least a week), then you can enjoy the rest of your summer to the fullest! Taking time to relax, be outside and just have fun is essential to decreasing stress and more importantly, enjoying life!

RESOURCES:

I love *Company's Coming* recipe books! You can usually find them at your grocery store. (If you live in Canada, Superstore always carries them at discount prices.) Otherwise, many are available online at Chapters or Amazon. Also, check out the *Company's Coming* website www.companyscoming.com. They have great FREE sample recipes in over 15 categories from slow cooker to grilling to beverages and desserts. Plus, you can order cookbooks directly from the site, although, with shipping, they are more expensive than buying in a store. While some of their older recipe books aren't the healthiest, they've done a great job with their newer ones. Here are a few of my favourites that include tasty and easy to prepare recipes (slow cooker, stove top and oven) that will make your life so much easier and healthier! Please note: I do not receive any benefits, financial or otherwise from *Company's Coming*. I just want to recommend these recipe options so hopefully they will help you as much as they've helped me!

1. *Company's Coming Healthy Slow Cooker*, 4th printing August, 2011.
2. *Company's Coming 5-Ingredient Slow Cooker Recipes*, 6th printing March, 2011.
3. *Company's Coming Chicken Now*, 1st printing May, 2007.
4. *Company's Coming Healthy in a Hurry: Eat Better in Under 30 Minutes*, 1st printing January, 2009.

Dr. Jennifer Harrison

CHAPTER 14: IS YOUR LAPTOP HURTING YOUR HEALTH?

Aren't laptops wonderful? They're light, easily portable between home and work or school, you can surf the net while watching TV or control your TV with your laptop. You can watch any show or movie you want, do your banking from the comfort of your favourite recliner and Skype or FaceTime with friends halfway around the world while sitting on the couch. However, did you know that laptops and other electronic devices like cell phones and tablets can actually be very harmful for your health? In this chapter I'll outline the hazards as well as offer some solutions so you can both take advantage of technology and minimize your health risks.

It's been interesting to see the emergence of more chronic health problems with my patients coinciding with the changes in technology. On the one hand, I can't imagine not having access to the internet and all the beneficial things that can come with it. However, as with most things, there is always a downside, and in the case of electronics, especially portable devices, the downsides are numerous and more dangerous than most people realize.

First of all, what most people don't understand is that laptops were never designed to be used as desktops. They were originally designed so that person from company A could go to company B and give a business presentation. Ergonomically, it's impossible to be in a healthy neutral posture position when you're working on a laptop. Over time, this leads to postural problems like tight neck and back muscles, neck and back pain, headaches, carpal tunnel syndrome, etc. And that's not even calculating in using cell phones, tablets and other portable electronic devices. All you have to do is take a look around you the next time you're at the mall or coffee shop. I can guarantee that you'll see people of all ages with their heads down, slouching, looking at the screen of their portable electronic device. Tragically, I'm now seeing neck and back

59

problems in children that I used to typically see in my 40-50 year old patients – all because of poor posture and spending too much time on laptops, tablets, cell phones and other portable electronic devices.

The second thing to be concerned about is radiation emission associated with wireless devices. On the one hand, isn't it great when you're travelling or shopping to be able to sign onto a free wireless service and check your email? However, this convenience is not without its health risks. In May, 2011, the World Health Organization (WHO) classified cell phones (and other wireless devices) as a category 2B risk, meaning a possible carcinogen due to radiation emission. In October, 2011, a spokesperson from Health Canada issued a similar warning with regard to risks to children. James McNamee stated, "Children are more sensitive to a variety of agents than adults as their brains and immune systems are still developing..."[1] Do you really want to put your children at risk by letting them play for endless hours on a wireless device instead of having them play outside?

Another thing to consider is addictions related to using the internet. Yes, this is a real diagnosable problem which has emerged over the past decade or so. In a 2009 article in the *Journal of Contemporary Psychotherapy*, Dr. Kimberly Young, a clinical psychologist and university professor, wrote that "Internet addiction is a new and often unrecognized clinical disorder that can cause relational, occupational, and social problems."[2] How many hours are you spending online every day? Do you ever go a day without checking your email or Facebook?

So, these are just a few of the health problems our wireless devices may be creating. Are there any solutions? Well, I'd like to propose a few.

1. Maintain neutral upright posture whenever you're using your laptop, cell phone, tablet or e-reader. If you are using your laptop as your main computer, get a keyboard and mouse for it and place your laptop on a riser essentially using it as a monitor. In other words, convert your laptop into a desk top.

2. Limit your time on wireless devices. When I'm working on my computer I set a timer for 30 minutes so that every half hour I step away from my laptop (yes, I have it set up as a desk top!) and do some stretches. Also, it's good to limit the amount of time per day that you spend using your electronic devices. This is even more important for children.

3. Get outside and connect with the earth! All living things have an electromagnetic field – grass, trees, soil, flowers, birds, and humans. The problem with the electromagnetic fields of wireless devices is that they're artificially created. However, there is growing research supporting the mental and physical health benefits of being and exercising outside. Yes, as long as you're somewhere where you can get a cell phone signal you'll still be exposed to "wireless pollution". However, the health benefits will help your body and mind be stronger and thus, able to deal with the variety of stressors our bodymind complexes are exposed to on a daily basis.

So while laptops and other portable electronic devices are here to stay, be sure to "unplug" every once in a while!

RESOURCES:

1. http://www.huffingtonpost.com/cris-rowan/10-reasons-why-handheld-devices-should-be-banned_b_4899218.html
2. Young, K. Internet Addiction: Diagnosis and Treatment Considerations. *J Comtemp Psychother* (2009) 39:241-246

Dr. Jennifer Harrison

CHAPTER 15: FIVE WAYS TO TURN A BAD DAY INTO A GREAT DAY

Bad days - we've all had them. Sometimes they even go from bad to worse. What if I told you that there are actually ways to turn those bad days around? In this chapter I'm going to show you five easy ways you can turn your next bad day into a great day.

Sometimes bad days just start out that way; you sleep through your alarm, you discover that your dog has chewed through your favourite pair of shoes you were going to wear to work or you go out and your car has a flat tire. Sometimes the day starts out OK but then you get some bad news, someone takes out their frustration on you or you spill coffee on yourself and don't have a change of clothes handy. Regardless of how your bad day got that way, there's a reason why it achieved momentum and ballooned out of control. However, by taking a few easy action steps, it is possible to turn your bad day into a good day, even a great one!

1. Stop and Breathe: One reason our bad days tend to spiral out of control is that we continue to feed the momentum. Something causes us to get upset or to be grumpy and that taints all other interactions and thoughts that we have throughout the day. A great way to slow down or change that momentum is to stop and take some deep breaths in and out. I like to use the mantra "Breathe in relaxation, breathe out tension". It's a simple but effective way to release stress, get grounded and enhance the blood circulation to your entire body, including your brain. It also gives you an opportunity to shift your focus.

2. Tap Out Your Cortices: This is a technique from the BodyTalk System. I introduced this technique in Chapter 2 and have mentioned it several times in this book already and for good reason. It works! The Cortices Technique helps to balance out the entire brain. It helps to enhance communication within and between the

63

hemispheres of your brain, balance out brain-body communication and it also helps to decrease stress. It only takes about 90 seconds to do and you can do it as many times a day as you need to. It's another simple way to help you move out of your bad day into a great one.

3. Music: We all have a favourite song that makes us feel good. It may have some happy memories attached to it or just the music and lyrics themselves help to shift our mood if we're feeling upset. Have some of your favourite songs handy on your iPod or cell phone. Sometimes just a couple of minutes of listening to some happy tunes is all it takes to start shifting the negative energy of a bad day.

4. Write It Down: If you're having a stressful day, write down what's bothering you. Don't hold back! It can be very cathartic to write down exactly how you're feeling about a certain situation or a particular person who is contributing to your bad day. Be sure to keep this information private or perhaps delete it after you've put your feelings into words so no one else can see it. However, by getting your frustration out of your head and onto paper (or onto your computer), you'll find that what's been triggering your bad day won't have as much steam as it had *before* you wrote things down.

5. Reflect: This may sound strange but sometimes the bad day we're having is actually a gift. That's right. The anger, frustration or sadness you may be experiencing might actually be there to give you a message or to help you realize that there are some changes you need to make in your life. We often experience repeated behaviour patterns (also known as getting into a rut) with work, our family and our relationships that aren't particularly helpful. At the end of the day, repeat steps 1 – 4 and then ask yourself these questions:

a) What's the life lesson in this for me?

b) What do I need to do differently so this person/situation doesn't have such a negative impact on me?

c) What do I need to do so I'm more resilient and this person/situation doesn't push me into a downward spiral? (The answer may be as simple as getting more sleep, drinking more water or getting outside more.)

You might not find all the answers right away, but by reflecting on these questions (or others you come up with yourself), you may gain insight as to what triggered you into having the bad day in the first place. It will also help to shift your energy and frame of mind so that you can change your bad day into a great day.

I hope you find these five steps a great way to Go From Your Stressed Self To Your Best Self™!

Dr. Jennifer Harrison

CHAPTER 16: ARE YOUR HABITS A HELP OR A HINDRANCE?

Over the years we all develop habits. Some we repeat daily, weekly, monthly and so on. I'd like you to stop for a moment and think about some of your habits:

1. What time you wake up in the morning.

2. When you shower – in the morning or before bed.

3. What you have for breakfast – if you have breakfast or not.

4. What route you take to work.

5. How many cups of coffee you have, how you take your coffee.

6. What you eat for snacks, lunch, supper.

7. Your workout routine – if you do exercise regularly.

8. What TV shows you watch or what video and computer games you play.

9. What time you go to bed.

All of these habits or repeated behavior patterns have been developed over time, in some cases weeks, in most cases years. Many basic habits, like brushing our teeth, we were taught as children by our parents.

So what happens in your brain and your body when you create a habit? Essentially you end up laying down a specific neural pathway in your brain. What does that mean? In your brain you have many brain cells or neurons that communicate with each other. When you repeat a behaviour or even a thought over and over again, the connections between all the neurons get stronger. The longer the behaviour is repeated, the stronger and more entrenched the neural pathway becomes. It's kind of like if there is a park or green space and you walk across it to get to the other side. If you do that once, you won't really see any difference in the grass. However, if you walk across in the same spot every day, pretty soon there will be a path that you can visibly see. If you were to repeat this action multiple times a day for many years, it would be equivalent to paving a path. It's this repetition that makes habits become engrained and easy to do. Now the challenge comes in determining whether the habit is helping you in your life or whether it's actually a hindrance.

So, what I'd like you to do is spend some time writing down your daily habits. Then I'd invite you to review the list and decide which ones are helping you in your life. Which ones contribute to your overall health, happiness and prosperity?

Then, I'd invite you to review the ones that are not helping – the ones that are a hindrance. Then ask yourself, what needs to happen to change these habits/repeated behaviour patterns that are hindering you from being as healthy and happy as you could be?

What I would recommend would be to pick one of these non-supportive habits and figure out how to change it. Where most people go wrong when they're wanting to make some positive changes in their lives is that they try to do too many new things at once. That's why most people – about 92 percent according to some studies – are not successful in keeping their New Year's resolutions.

We've probably all heard of the saying that it takes 21 days to create a new habit. This is actually a MYTH![1] That's right. The so called 21-day rule was actually something that was written in a book from the 1960s by a plastic surgeon who observed that for most people it took about 21 days for them to become accustomed to how they looked after having had plastic surgery. For some reason, this got misinterpreted and the "21-day rule" became gospel.

What newer research actually showed was that, on average, it took about 66 days to create a simple habit like drinking a glass of water after breakfast. And this is just the average. For some people it only took about 18 days for this to become an automatic behaviour or habit. For others it took an estimated 254 days! So there's a high degree of variation from one person to another when it comes to forming a new habit.

The key thing with creating a new helpful or supportive habit is the same thing that happened to create the old non-supportive habit. REPETITION!

So when you're creating a helpful habit, be kind to yourself, be consistent, cheer yourself on and give yourself credit. This kind of positive reinforcement helps to lay down the new neural pathway that you're creating in your brain. If you miss a few days, get right back on track as soon as possible. Once this new habit, like exercising regularly for example, starts to become comfortable and familiar, consider working on creating the next new helpful habit.

Slow and steady wins the race when it comes to breaking old habits and creating new ones. Remember, around 66 days. It's these helpful habits that help you Go From Your Stressed Self To Your Best Self™!

RESOURCES:

1. http://www.huffingtonpost.com/james-clear/forming-new-habits_b_5104807.html

Dr. Jennifer Harrison

CHAPTER 17: SIX EASY SOLUTIONS TO SIX TIME WASTING PROBLEMS

When I saw organizational expert Jill Pollack interviewed on TV outlining the actual amount of time people waste doing everyday activities, I was blown away. What amazed me even more was that the solutions to these problems were very simple. Like I talked about in the previous chapter, it's all about asking, are your habits a help or a hindrance? Wasting time and being surrounded by clutter increase our stress. Below are the six issues Jill Pollack spoke about and the effective solutions she offered to solve the problem of needlessly wasting time and resources.

1. On average, people spend six minutes per day looking for their keys.

Solution: Hang a key hook rack or get a bowl to set on a table at the entrance of your home where you automatically put the keys when you come home. This simple solution could save you about three hours per month – the length of two movies – in wasted time that you could be putting to better use. Also, hunting for misplaced keys is a sure-fire way to increase your stress level – needlessly.

2. The average Canadian family washes over 400 loads of laundry per year, a lot of which involves wasted time, energy and resources washing clothes that don't necessarily need washing.

Solution: Set up wall hooks for clothes that have only been worn once (not clean but not dirty), so they don't end up on the floor. Then, after they've been worn a second time, they can go into the laundry hamper. This way you won't end up wasting time or water doing unnecessary extra loads of laundry.

3. Women without shoe racks are seven times more likely to be late for work.

Solution: Use a shoe organizer!

4. Eighty percent of what we keep we never use.

Solution: Use memorabilia boxes for clothing and other items that have sentimental value to you. Use organizational boxes for stuff you do use regularly. Be sure to keep them separate. You can also take photos of items that have sentimental value and create a special photo album or scrap book while getting rid of the actual items themselves.

5. The average Canadian household has more than $300 in unused gift cards. That's free shopping!

Solution: Get a separate change purse for gift cards or store credit vouchers.

6. Eleven percent of people don't know where their Social Insurance Number (SIN) cards are.

Solution: Make copies of important documents like SIN cards, birth certificates, passports, etc. and put them in a safe deposit box or a fireproof safe.

I hope Jill's solutions help you free up more time so you can do the things you enjoy! Being organized goes a long way in decreasing stress which, in turn, helps to create a happier and healthier you!

RESOURCES:

1. Jill Pollock, Professional Organizer as interviewed on *The Marilyn Denis Show* June 24, 2013. https://www.youtube.com/watch?v=8vzTbzFXkUE

CHAPTER 18: HOW TO AVOID THE TOP FIVE TIME AND ENERGY WASTERS

In this chapter I'm going to outline the top five things we regularly do that actually end up wasting our time, draining us of energy and causing undo stress. These activities may seem innocent enough. They may even make us feel like we're actually accomplishing something, but they are really energy wasters in disguise. I'll also provide some easy solutions so that you're making the most of your time while also taking care of your health.

1. Channel surfing: It wasn't that many years ago, especially if you lived in a rural area, that you only had access to a handful of TV channels. Now you have the option of literally hundreds of channels. So with all those options, isn't it amazing that you can still surf through dozens of programs and not really find anything worth watching? How often, at the end of a long day, do you plop yourself on the couch, pick up the remote and start randomly going through the channels? While you may think that you're relaxing, you're actually stimulating your brain with one snippet of information after another, after another. If you can't find a show that is engaging and enhancing your life somehow through knowledge, humour or entertainment, you'd be much better off taking the 30 minutes or longer you spend channel surfing to exercise or meditate instead. Even tapping out your Cortices will balance out your brain, your bodymind connections and relax you more effectively than 30 minutes of channel surfing. Deep breathing for five minutes will be more beneficial. Going for a 15 minute walk will be healthier. Are you seeing a pattern here? When you come home from a long day and want to unwind, I would recommend doing the Cortices technique as soon as you step in the house. I would recommend doing it again before you sit down to watch TV. If you don't already have a specific program in mind to watch, then I would give yourself a time limit, say five minutes or less, to find a single program worth watching. If you can't find

Dr. Jennifer Harrison

one, then it would be much healthier to exercise, do a breathing meditation, or read a book. That way, you won't be wasting time and you'll actually be doing something positive for yourself and not letting your precious energy get sucked out of you.

2. Facebook and Twitter: We all know the value of social media in staying connected with family and friends. However, it can also be insidious. One minute you're catching up and then the next thing you know, you've gone down the rabbit hole and a hour or more has passed by as you got pulled into checking out random bits of information. Set a time limit of 30 minutes by using the timer on your cell phone or watch. You shouldn't be sitting for more than 30 minutes at a time anyway as it's bad for your back and overall health. This way you can get in to post/tweet what you want, check in on family and friends and not waste your precious time.

3. YouTube: Although there are a lot of questionable videos on YouTube, there is a lot of great stuff on there, too. (See "Chapter 33: Get Fit for Free".) However, as we've all experienced, it's easy to get pulled into video surfing and wasting a lot of time. Again, unless you're looking for something specific, like some TED talks, set your timer for 30 minutes to browse through YouTube. Even if you are watching something that will be an hour long, set your timer anyway so that every 30 minutes you're standing up to stretch for a minute before sitting down again.

4. Shopping online: There's no question about the benefits of online shopping. You can get customer reviews before you make your purchase, you can see what's out there and compare prices. If you live in a rural area, you don't have to make a trip to the big city to get items that you can't get in your home town. If you do live in a big city, you can do your research before you actually go out to buy your item and save yourself from driving all over the place to find what you want. However, shopping online can also be a big time waster, especially if you don't have a specific item in mind and you're actually just "window shopping". Again, whether you're searching for a specific item or you just want to see the latest and greatest, set a time limit of 30 minutes so you don't end up wasting hours in front of your computer when you could be doing other things that are healthier and more productive.

5. Email: I can't imagine being without email now. However, it can suck up a lot of time and energy that could be spent better elsewhere. My strategy is to go in and clear out my Junk Mail folder first while double checking to make sure there aren't any emails in there that should have gone into my Inbox. Then I "triage" my emails, opening and responding to the ones that need my attention first. Then I go back and deal with the others. I have to admit that in the past couple of years, I've gotten behind in reading email newsletters from some of the websites to which I subscribe. One strategy is to put these types of emails into a general folder that you can create for all your newsletters, or into individual folders for each newsletter. Then, set aside time once or twice a week to just look at the newsletters. Again, set a time limit. If you need more than 30 minutes to go through emails, make sure that you set a timer to go off every 30 minutes so you can get up and stretch or tap out your Cortices.

Our time and energy are valuable and so is our health. It's all too precious to be wasted. I hope these recommendations help you to manage and enjoy your time.

Dr. Jennifer Harrison

CHAPTER 19: HOW TO BE A BETTER YOU

Very few of us are truly happy with ourselves. There's always something that we feel we need to work on or change. If you go to your favorite online bookstore, you can find literally tens of thousands of self-improvement books. You can learn about ways to become more confident, more forgiving, more outgoing, more joyful, more prosperous, more attractive, more successful, more spiritual, and the list goes on and on. Many of the books are extremely helpful, others less so. However, in this chapter, I want to show you a simple way to be a "better" you. You might be surprised to find out you don't have to change as much as you think!

Here's a simple exercise that I want you to do:

1. How do you feel about yourself? On a scale of 1 to 10, with 1 being very unhappy with yourself and 10 being extremely satisfied, how would you rate how you feel?

Get a pen and paper or sit at your computer and write down five things you really like about yourself. Be honest! Things you might write could be "I like that I have a great smile" or it might be "I like that I am a great organizer". Just write down five things starting with the words, "I like that I …..".

2. Now re-write the sentences replacing the word "like" with "love" by writing "I love that I…..".

3. Next, go stand in front of a mirror, look at yourself, smile and say each of those statements out loud.

4. Compare how you felt before you started the exercise with how you feel now.

Sometimes we need to remind ourselves of how great we already are! That doesn't mean that there isn't room for personal growth. However, always focusing on the things we feel we need to change perpetuates an underlying belief system that there is always something wrong with us. There is great power in focusing on the good stuff that's already there, to be mindful, grateful, and focused on "what is" instead of always concentrating on what you think you have to change. A great way to be a "better" you is to practice self-appreciation and self-love. Remember, a happier you is a healthier you!

CHAPTER 20: AN ATTITUDE OF GRATITUDE - DOES IT MAKE A DIFFERENCE TO YOUR HEALTH?

As children, we were taught to say "Thank you" when something was given to us or someone did something nice for us. In recent years, the self-help gurus have been guaranteeing that our desires will be manifested more quickly if we have an "attitude of gratitude". Does being grateful really make a difference? Does our health actually benefit from having an attitude of gratitude?

There is a relatively new area of research called Positive Psychology, where scientists have been exploring the effects of gratitude on people's outlook on life and even the physical effects of practicing feeling grateful. One study that was published in 2014 looked at whether positive psychological interventions, such as engaging in good deeds and writing gratitude letters, made a difference with patients having symptoms of depression. The pilot study, titled "Happiness intervention decreases pain and depression, boosts happiness among primary care patients." was six weeks long and involved follow up sessions up to six months later. What they found was that scores improved from the baseline (taken before the study started) to the six month follow up in areas of health, vitality, mental health and the effects of mental and physical health on daily activities.[1]

Dr. Alex Korb is a postdoctoral researcher at UCLA (University of California Los Angeles). In a blog he wrote for *Psychology Today* Dr. Korb says, "One study by a couple of American researchers assigned young adults to keep a daily journal of things they were grateful for (Emmons and McCullough, 2003). They assigned other groups to journal about things that annoyed them, or reasons why they were better off than others. The young adults assigned to keep gratitude journals showed greater increases in determination, attention, enthusiasm and energy compared to the other groups. While that shows a clear benefit of gratitude, it also makes a clear distinction. Realizing that other people are worse off than you is not gratitude. Gratitude requires an appreciation of the positive aspects of your situation."[2]

In another study by the same researches, following the identical format except with adults, they found that people who kept a weekly gratitude journal had greater improvements on exercise patterns and even had a reduction in some of their physical aches and pains![2]

Other research done in China found that "higher levels of gratitude were associated with better sleep, and with lower anxiety and depression."[2]

So clearly, it appears that being grateful does indeed have a positive impact on various aspects of your health. The question is, how do you apply this information to your life? Easy! Every day spend time either writing down the things that you are grateful for or even just spend time thinking about what you really appreciate in your life. However, the key is not to just think about what you are grateful for, you have to focus on *feeling* the gratitude. What a simple but powerful way to enhance our lives! Imagine the difference it would make if children and teenagers were taught in school to keep gratitude journals and were encouraged to actually develop an attitude of gratitude. It would indeed change the world!

RESOURCES:

1. http://www.ncbi.nlm.nih.gov/pubmed/24451155
2. http://www.psychologytoday.com/blog/prefrontal-nudity/201211/the-grateful-brain

CHAPTER 21: NOVEMBER IS PEACE MONTH

On November 11, every year, Canada and many other countries around the world, observe Remembrance Day (also called Veterans' Day and Armistice Day) with services and a moment of silence at 11 am. It was at the 11th hour on the 11th day of the 11th month, 1918, that a treaty was signed to end WWI. While World War I was supposed to be "the war to end all wars", this obviously hasn't been the case. However, that doesn't mean that peace is not possible. I love the quote by Mother Teresa: "What can you do to promote world peace? Go home and love your family." This also includes loving yourself!

In this chapter I'm going to share some peace affirmations I created for you. Affirmations are positive statements that can be used to reinforce an existing belief or to create a new one. They can be helpful in shifting your perspective and in achieving your goals. The affirmations I'm going to share with you are designed to help create more peace in your life.

1. As I breathe in peace, I breathe out stress.

2. My heart fills with peace as I focus on the people I love.

3. I create peace by meditating every day.

4. I feel peaceful when I spend time in nature.

5. I intentionally create peaceful places in my home.

6. As I relax my body and quiet my mind, I create peace within me.

7. I listen to peaceful music every day.

8. The more peaceful I feel, the more I am surrounded by peace in all areas of my life.

9. I feel peaceful when I make time to do the things I love to do.

81

Dr. Jennifer Harrison

10. I am grateful for all the peace in my life.

I also created a YouTube video with these affirmations. You can access it on my YouTube channel:
https://www.youtube.com/watch?v=DSPr5bFsp7Q

As you watch the video, you can say the affirmations out loud, or silently in your head.

Intentionally making time each day to create peace in your life is a great way to Go From Your Stressed Self To Your Best Self™!

CHAPTER 22: HOW TO EXPERIENCE PEACE AND JOY THIS HOLIDAY SEASON

Despite the fact that we sing Christmas Carols like *Joy to the World* and *Silent Night* lyrics like "sleep in heavenly peace", often times the holiday season is anything but filled with joy and peace. Between school pageants, office Christmas parties, shopping for gifts, not to mention the extra cooking and baking for the family, it's pretty easy to get stressed out. However, in this chapter I'm going to share with you a few simple things that you can do so that you really can experience peace and joy this holiday season.

1. Tap out your Cortices! The Cortices Technique is one of the techniques from the BodyTalk System and is an effective way to decrease stress. Please refer to Chapter 2.

2. Do breathing meditations. Often times when I mention doing meditation the first thing my patients say is, "Oh, I can't do that! I can't get my brain to stop." No problem! There are many different types of meditation (Please refer to Chapter 1) and if you're new to meditating or like most people, you have trouble getting your brain to quieten down, do a breathing meditation. All you have to do is sit quietly for a moment and co-ordinate your breathing with a simple mantra or repeating sentence. Here are a couple that I like to use: Inhale saying in your mind, "As I breathe in peace", then exhale saying in your mind "I breathe out tension." Repeat this sequence at least 5-10 times until you feel yourself start to relax. Another one I use is, "As I breathe in joy, I breathe out stress." This is a simple stress reliever that you can do if you're taking the bus or stopped at a red light or even at your desk at work. I've even used these when I've been stuck in a long line up at the grocery store!

3. Be grateful! Expressing and feeling gratitude is a powerful way to shift your energy toward experiencing peace and joy. Before you eat a meal or snack, take a moment to be grateful that you have healthy food to eat and clean water to drink. If things start getting stressful at work, stop and be grateful that you have a job. If you're stuck in rush hour traffic, stop and be grateful for your car. Think about your family and your friends and other things you appreciate in your life. Be grateful! It's a wonderful way to generate peace and joy in your life.

4. Listen to your favourite music. Hum or sing along! If you haven't done this already, have your favourite CDs handy or a playlist set up on your iPod or other portable device. Listening to music can help stimulate your brain in a specific way. There's even research that shows that water (remember we're made up of at least 70 percent water) forms crystals differently depending on whether it is exposed to relaxing music or heavy metal music.[1]

5. Be mindful of the TV shows and movies you watch plus the material you read. During stressful times, it's beneficial to expose yourself to "gentle" media that's not too violent or suspenseful. Minimize your exposure to the news. Most times, the news reports are focused on the horrible things that are happening in the world. Many times, the reports are based on pure speculation designed to promote fear. If you need to find out what's happening in the world, just go online to a media news outlet and scan the headlines. If there is information you absolutely need to know, then do a Google search. Otherwise, be gentle with yourself so you can focus on creating peace and joy in your life.

I hope you find these suggestions helpful. Remember, the only way for you to truly experience peace and joy this holiday season is for *you* to intentionally create it.

RESOURCES:

1. Emoto, Masaru. *The Hidden Messages in Water.* Hillsboro, Oregon: Beyond Words Publishing, 2004.

CHAPTER 23: 'TIS THE SEASON TO BE...

Well, according to the Christmas carol, "Tis the season to be jolly". And, for many people it will be a happy time of holidays, travel, wonderful meals with family and friends, and pleasant memories of Christmas past. However, sometimes I find that the holiday season can be a time for magnifying things that maybe aren't so jolly. I know Christmas this year, for me, will be a mixed bag of joy and sadness. My Dad passed away earlier this year (2013) and the anniversary of my Mom's passing is New Year's Day. While I'm definitely going to be happy to see family and friends when I travel home for Christmas, I know there will be some sadness and grief, too. I also know that my story is not unique. Many of my patients and other people I know are in the same boat. So, what are we to do with this clash of the media and movies telling us that we're supposed to be happy during this magical time of year and our own hearts telling us a different story? Well, in this chapter I want to share with you some ideas of things we can do so that we can be true to our hearts *and* celebrate the joy of the season.

1. Journal: Writing down your thoughts and emotions can definitely help to alleviate some of the heaviness in your heart and clutter in your mind. It can also help to add clarity to what you're going through and be an important part of the journey. If you're new to journaling and don't know where to start, begin with asking yourself, "How am I feeling right now?" and "What is causing me to feel this way?"

2. Browse Through Photo Albums and Old Family Videos: Allow the memories to come back and let yourself have a good laugh and a good cry. Energetically our hearts hold onto many strong emotions. In Chinese medicine the heart is seen to process joy and sadness as two sides of the same coin.

Dr. Jennifer Harrison

3. Blue Christmas Services: Depending on your religious or spiritual affiliation, many churches have what is called a Blue Christmas service. This is a special (usually evening) service for people
who may have lost a loved one during the year or who may be
experiencing a difficult time with their health or other troubles.
It's a way of acknowledging that Christmas isn't necessarily a
happy time for everyone. It's also a safe and loving way to express
your sadness, or whatever emotion you may be experiencing,
while providing some peace.

Remember, if you are really struggling emotionally, you may need
to see your medical doctor, a psychologist or counselor for help.

4. Create New Christmas Memories: If some of your past Christmas memories are far from happy ones, focus on creating new joyful Christmas memories! Make a list of things you like to do that
make you happy and that you enjoy. Then, take action! If you love
Christmas lights, then check to see if there are some tours or special displays in your area. One year when I was home visiting my
family, we went on a lovely horse drawn hay ride around town
looking at everyone's Christmas lights. If you love music, there
are always Christmas concerts or pageants to attend, many of
them free or for a small donation. If you love the outdoors, get a
group of friends together for snow shoeing or skiing and then plan
a potluck afterwards. If the indoors is more your style, plan a
games night with some family and friends.

Remember, the past is the past. It doesn't mean that it doesn't
need to be addressed, but there's nothing like focusing on the present and creating a season that truly is jolly!

SECTION 2: NUTRITION

Dr. Jennifer Harrison

CHAPTER 24: THE BASICS - WATER

In this chapter I want to talk to you about something that is essential to every living thing on the planet, that every cell in your body needs, and something that most people are seriously lacking. That's right, WATER!

Every single cell in your body needs water in order to bring nutrients into the cell and to carry cell waste products out of the cell. In other words, water is responsible for bringing in the good stuff as well as taking out the trash. When your brain is fully hydrated, it is approximately 80 percent water. Your blood is made up of about 80 percent water. Even the discs between the vertebrae (bones) in your spine contain water. In fact, the water content of discs is about 90 percent at birth and decreases to about 70 percent by the fifth decade. So, you can see how water is important for so many things in your body. On the flip side, can you see how your health can be negatively affected over time by not drinking enough water?

Let's see if you're getting enough water, check some signs that may indicate that you're not and look at a few action steps you can take to make sure you and your family are well hydrated.

1. How do you know if you're drinking enough water? Well, one thing that you cannot rely on is how thirsty you are. By the time you feel thirsty, you are already dehydrated. A more reliable indicator is the colour of your urine. If it is darker yellow or amber in colour, that indicates you definitely need more water. If it is mostly clear, that is an indicator that you are well hydrated. (Please note, that taking a multivitamin or vitamin B supplements can make your urine bright yellow in colour.)

2. Besides just not drinking enough water, the following are diuretics or what I call "water vampires". They can literally suck the water out of you and cause you to be dehydrated:

Soft drinks, many with caffeine and sodium

Coffee and tea, both with high levels of caffeine

Alcohol

Sports drinks, with high sodium and sugar content, not to mention artificial flavors and colours

Energy Drinks with high levels caffeine, and a number of other chemicals

3. Here are some of the health problems that can occur over the short term, and long term, from not drinking enough water:

Headaches: I had a patient, we'll call him Scott, who came to see me several years ago. His story is a common one that I see in my practice. He had been having headaches almost daily for a couple of years for which he'd been taking Tylenol. It turned out that he was only drinking water once a week after he played hockey. The rest of the time he was drinking coffee, juice or pop. I did a physical exam but couldn't find anything significant physically that was contributing to his headaches, except for the fact that he was chronically dehydrated. I told him about the importance of water and how much he should be drinking each day. Over a couple of weeks he gradually increased his water intake. Two weeks later he came in to see me and said his headaches were gone! I said, "That's great, Scott, but do you realize all the Tylenol (which is toxic to the liver) that you've taken daily over the past two years wasn't what your body needed? All your body needed was water?" His eyes widened in shock because he hadn't made that connection yet.

Fatigue and irritability: Mild to moderate dehydration can cause you to feel tired and less alert. This can impact your concentration and work effectiveness, not to mention create safety hazards if you are driving or doing something that requires your full attention. Dehydrated people often aren't fun to be around because of irritability.

Constipation: In order to have a healthy digestive system, you need to be getting enough fibre *and* water.

Urinary Tract Infections: Not drinking enough water results in decreased urine output as well as darker coloured urine. Urine helps to get rid of waste products we don't need. The actual flow of urine through the urethra helps to clear out bacteria. If there is a decreased output and flow of urine, you could be more predisposed to getting a urinary tract infection.

Muscle Cramps: Not drinking enough water on a hot day or when you've been exercising can lead to painful muscle cramps. Also, long term dehydration can lead to tight connective tissue and general muscle pain. Any Registered Massage Therapist or manual therapist can tell very quickly if their client is a healthy water drinker or not, just by touching their skin and muscles.

Neck and Back Pain: As I mentioned above, the discs in your spine, when healthy, contain 70 – 90 percent water. However, some research indicates chronic lack of water over time can cause the discs to degenerate, which in turn, can lead to neck and back pain.

4. So, how much water should you be drinking? We lose about 2L of fluids every day through breathing, sweating, urinating and defecating. According to the Mayo Clinic, The Institute of Medicine determined that an adequate intake (AI) for men is roughly 3 liters (about 13 cups) of total beverages a day. The AI for women is 2.2 liters (about 9 cups) of total beverages a day. While we can obtain some fluids through our food (especially from watery food such as watermelon and tomatoes), we need to get fluid from other sources. Now, they go on to say that juice and milk count as fluids. However, they recommend that the bulk of your fluid intake

Dr. Jennifer Harrison

should be water because it's calorie-free, inexpensive and readily available.[1]

According to Australian research, the recommended daily amount of fluids (including milk, juice and water) for children is:[2]

5 glasses (1 litre) for 5 to 8 year olds

7 glasses (1.5 litres) for 9 to12 year olds

8 to 10 glasses (2 litres) for 13+ years

If your physical activity includes sports or exercise where you're sweating a lot, you will need to increase this amount. Again, use the colour of your urine as an indicator of how well you're hydrated.

5. A common complaint I get from my patients is that they don't like the taste of water. If you fall into this category, here are several simple solutions to make water taste great:

Add a little bit of lemon or lime juice to your water.

Add a wedge of frozen orange, lemon or lime to your water.

If you prefer hot beverages, you can drink just hot water or hot water with lemon or lime.

Sometimes I'll have a glass of sparkling water, either plain or with a little bit of lemon or lime juice added, just for a change.

I hope this chapter has illustrated how essential water is for your overall health and well-being and how, with just a little bit of effort, you can make sure that you and your family are getting the amount of water they need to be happy and healthy.

RESOURCES:

1. http://www.mayoclinic.com/health/water/NU00283

2. http://www.healthykids.nsw.gov.au/kids-teens/choose-water-as-a-drink-kids.aspx
3. http://www.mayoclinic.org/healthy-lifestyle/nutrition-and-healthy-eating/in-depth/water/art-20044256?pg=2

Dr. Jennifer Harrison

CHAPTER 25: THE SKINNY ON CARBS

OK, I have a multiple choice question for you. Which of the following would be considered to be "carbs", meaning carbohydrates?

a) A carrot
b) An apple
c) Brown rice
d) A raisin oatmeal cookie
e) All of the above

Recently, I've noticed more and more of my patients telling me that they've "cut out carbs" from their diet. When I ask them to be more specific, they usually say bread, cookies, crackers and chips. This has led me to realize that there is a lot of confusion about carbs and indeed downright misconceptions about what carbohydrates are, what they do to and for our bodies and which foods actually fall under the category of carbs.

Well, in case you weren't sure, the correct answer to the multiple choice question was e) All of the above. By definition, "carbohydrates include sugars, glycogen (stored form of carbohydrates in animals), starches and cellulose."[1] To break it down further, carbohydrate groups include:

1. Simple sugars (monosaccharides) like glucose, fructose (found in fruits), galactose (found in milk) and others.

2. Disaccharides like table sugar and milk sugar.

3. Polysaccharides like glycogen, which is how carbohydrates are stored in animals including humans, and starch which is the stored form of carbs in plants including veggies and dietary fibre like cellulose, for example, which is the part of the cell walls of plants which can't be digested by humans but helps to move food through the intestines.

So what does this mean? Well, it means that carbohydrates are found in fruits, vegetables, whole grains, nuts and dairy products like milk, cheese and yogurt. It also means that any processed foods made with these products contain carbohydrates. For example, the raisin oatmeal cookie mentioned above (assuming it was from a traditional recipe) would contain a variety of carbs from different sources such as the oatmeal, processed flour, table sugar, sugars in the butter and milk and from the raisins.

A question you may now be asking is, "I thought carbs were bad for you?" Well, there are some important things you need to know about carbohydrates.

1. There are GOOD carbs and BAD carbs. Good carbs would be in the form of fruits, veggies, nuts and whole grains as well as milk products such as low fat cheese, yogurt and butter. Good carbs generally are also nutrient rich, meaning they contain important vitamins and minerals. Some of you may be questioning the health benefits of butter and cheese. However, unless you have allergies, intolerances or a specific health condition that prohibits the intake of milk and dairy products, butter, cheese and yogurt in low quantities can be healthy for you. These products are, in fact, recommended by the Canada Food Guide, the USDA My Plate and other sources.

2. Bad carbs generally come in the form of processed foods that are low in or void of healthy nutrients. This would include chips, nachos, tacos, candy, chocolate bars, pop, sugary drinks, and anything made with processed white flour like white bread, cookies, cakes and donuts. In other words, "junk food".

3. There has been a lot of hype recently about whole wheat and whole grains being very bad for you and for your brain. There is no question that in North America we eat way too much bread, not to mention processed foods. Some people have actual food sensitivities or are Celiac and it is unhealthy for them to eat anything with wheat or grains containing gluten. They need to choose whole grains such as quinoa, buckwheat, amaranth, etc. However, the key with grains, or with any carbohydrate for that matter, is that you need to be eating it in combination with a form of healthy fat and protein. Carbohydrates, with the exception of dietary fibre, gets broken down into simple sugars or glucose. Every carbohydrate has a glycemic index which refers to how quickly it gets converted to glucose in the body. The faster it gets converted to sugar in the body, the higher the glycemic index. That's why eating a chocolate bar gives you a "sugar high" which is then followed later by a "sugar crash". This is very unhealthy for your body, especially if this is a typical eating pattern. Over time, it can contribute to the development of Type II diabetes. However, if you make sure that you're eating good carbs in combination with a healthy fat and protein, then that will help keep your blood sugars from spiking which will benefit your whole body. An example would be having a salmon and lettuce sandwich made with whole grain bread. A healthy snack would be an apple with some almonds.

So the next time you're thinking about getting rid of carbs from your diet, focus on getting rid of the *bad* carbs and make sure that, whether at meal time or snack time, you're combining the good carbs with a healthy fat and protein.

RESOURCES:

1. Tortora, Gerard J., Derrickson, Bryan. *Principles of Anatomy and Physiology* (11th ed.), Hoboken, NJ: John Wiley & Sons, Inc., 2006. pp. 44-45.
2. http://www.hc-sc.gc.ca/fn-an/food-guide-aliment/index-eng.php
3. http://celiacdisease.about.com/od/theglutenfreediet/a/Gluten GrainQs.htm
4. http://www.celiac.com/categories/Gluten-Free--Grains--and-- Flours-c-3384

Dr. Jennifer Harrison

CHAPTER 26: HEALTHY NUTRITION ON THE GO

While it's actually unhealthy to be eating on the go (our digestive systems function best when we are relaxed when we eat), there are ways to ensure that you have healthy food on hand for those extra-busy days. In this chapter I've gathered some great resources for you that will show you how you can easily create healthy nutrition on the go. This will help to keep you healthy and functioning at your best throughout your day!

The USDA (United States Department of Agriculture) created a program called Choose My Plate a few years ago in an effort to help Americans fight obesity and make healthier food choices.[1] The following is a short YouTube video aimed at showing kids (and adults) how easy and effective it is to prepare fruit and veggie snack boxes that are both nutritious and portable:

https://www.youtube.com/watch?v=AGrczY8AMJc

In order to keep blood sugar levels from spiking (remember the sugar high is inevitably followed by a sugar crash), it's important to combine protein in with all your snacks. Suggestions for portable protein include peanut butter, nuts and hummus. Number 2 under Resources is a link to a great article listing 31 portable high protein snacks.

Preparing healthy snacks to take with you to work, school or on your road trip is an excellent way to be healthy and to maximize your energy to deal with whatever life has in store for you. In other words, it's a great way to Go From Your Stressed Self To Your Best Self™!

RESOURCES:

1. http://www.choosemyplate.gov/kids/VideosSongs.html
2. http://greatist.com/health/high-protein-snacks-portable

Dr. Jennifer Harrison

CHAPTER 27: THE TOP FIVE SUMMERTIME FRUITS

Although we have fruit available to us all year round, there's something wonderful about summertime fruits. They're fresh, they're in season and they appeal to the five senses. However, in addition to all this, they're also super healthy for you! Here's a list of my top five summertime fruit picks and why you might want to put them at the top of your list, too.

Watermelon: Who doesn't have fun summertime memories of eating watermelon outside and seeing who could spit the seeds the farthest? Well, in addition to wonderful memories and great taste, watermelon, as the name suggests, is a great source of water. In fact, it's 92 percent water. It also is high in vitamin A, potassium and magnesium. Research has shown that watermelon contains high amounts of lycopene which is a powerful anti-oxidant. Lycopene has been shown to reduce the incidence of certain cancers as well as heart disease. Plus, one cup of watermelon only has 50 calories!

Pineapple: Of course this fruit always conjures up images of tropical islands, whether it's winter or summer. Pineapple is also a good source of vitamin C which helps with your immune system. It also contains manganese which is a mineral that helps with connective tissue health and balances histamine levels which get high during allergic reactions. Pineapple has an enzyme called bromelain which has been shown to help with arthritis pain by decreasing inflammation. It's also low in calories with one cup of pineapple only having 77 calories.

Kiwi fruit: A gift from "Down Under", kiwi are a good source of vitamins A and C. In fact, a medium kiwi has more vitamin C than an orange! They are also a good source of fiber which is important in preventing colon cancer. A medium kiwi has only 46 calories.

Dr. Jennifer Harrison

Blueberries: Well, of course, blueberries are well known for their antioxidant properties. This is because they are rich in vitamin A and manganese. Blueberries are also valued for their antiviral activity. One cup of blueberries has only 82 calories.

Cherries: Another wonderful summertime fruit, cherries are very rich in vitamin A (over twice as much as blueberries) as well as potassium which can help lower blood pressure. One cup of cherries has 104 calories.

"Apples, peaches, pears and plums, tell me when your birthday comes." I got this little ditty from one of my nutrition course instructors at Chiropractic College. It is a fun reminder of the fruits that are good sources of soluble fiber which is great in managing cholesterol levels.

So, whether it's summer, fall, winter or spring, it's important to make sure fruit is part of your diet every day. For more healthy fruit options, check out the *Canadian Living* article under Resources.

RESOURCES:

1. http://www.canadianliving.com/health/nutrition/top_25_healthy_fruits_blueberries_apples_cherries_bananas_and_21_more_healthy_picks.php
2. Dunne, Lavon J. *Nutrition Almanac* (5th ed.), New York: McGraw-Hill, 2002.

CHAPTER 28: YOU ARE HOW YOU EAT

We're all familiar with the old adage "You are what you eat." Of course this is absolutely true. Everything we eat goes to fuel our bodies so we can do all our daily activities from working to working out to doing the actual grocery shopping. The food we consume also goes to help our bodies to heal from illnesses and injuries as well as to rejuvenate from the wear and tear of daily living. Naturally, the quality and quantity of food we eat helps determines our energy levels and overall health. However, what most people don't realize is that it's also very important to be aware of *how* you eat. Are you always in a rush when you eat? Do you skip meals because you're too busy to eat? Do you plop your kids in front of their favorite cartoon in the morning so that they'll sit still long enough to eat breakfast? Do you have your lunch in front of your computer while you check your email and Facebook? Has sitting in front of the TV become the standard way of how you and your family eat supper every night? If you've answered "Yes" to any or all of the above questions then this is the chapter for you! Even if you are conscious about eating healthy foods, find out how you may be harming yourself and your family by not being aware of *how* you are eating.

Our nervous system has different modes. One mode is known as the "fight, freeze or flight" or stress mode. The other is the "rest, digest and restore" or relaxation mode. I have discussed previously that when we get stuck in stress mode for extended periods of time, even if it is at a low level, it can have a negative impact on our health. I have also talked about the importance of being in the relaxed or "rest, digest and restore" mode and how that benefits our health and helps us to heal and rejuvenate our bodymind complex. Well, there is a reason it's called "rest and digest" mode. Your bodymind can only properly digest food when you are in rest, digest and restore mode. When we're in fight or flight mode, the body is preparing itself for just that – to fight or to flee. Over time, eating in a rush and skipping meals can lead to digestive system problems like reflux (aka GERD – gastroesophageal reflux disease), bloating, gas, diarrhea and constipation. Poor eating habits have also been linked to obesity which in turn is associated with all sorts of other health issues like diabetes, heart disease and early death.

So what happens to your digestive system when you are in fight or flight mode? Well, a whole bunch of things. There is a decrease in blood flow to your stomach and intestines, there is a decrease in the production of hormones and enzymes that help you to digest your food and there is a decrease in the movement of food and the ability to absorb nutrients from your food. Also, chronic stress affects our adrenal glands by causing them to continually produce cortisol for extended periods of time. It's been shown that chronically high cortisol levels can be associated with weight gain.[1]

So, when you are in stress mode, how is your body supposed to properly digest your food, let alone absorb the nutrients that will help you deal with your stress? That's right, it can't! This is a discussion I often have with my patients. When we eat, we need to be conscious about setting aside some quiet time. That means that you're not texting, checking emails or your favorite social media site. (I need to remind myself of this from time to time, too!) It also means you're not driving while you're eating. I remember several years ago hearing an ad on the radio about a popular fast food chain that was advertising that they had changed the wrapping of their food so you could drive and eat at the same time! Yikes! In the past few years, many places have implemented safe driving laws that prohibit you from eating and driving and being a distracted driver. Eating your lunch should not be hazardous to your health let alone to those around you! Sounds logical, but not everyone gets that.

Parents also don't realize the negative impact they're having on their children's health by essentially teaching them that it's OK to eat while watching TV or modeling unhealthy behavior like skipping meals. They're basically setting their children up for a lifetime of digestive system problems.

An interesting study done of middle-aged women in New Zealand suggested that people who eat too quickly tend to have a higher body mass index (BMI).[2] BMI is used as a health indicator taking into account your height and weight. A high BMI is generally associated with being overweight or obese. Interestingly, another study showed that when families eat together, teenaged boys tended to have lower BMIs.[3]

So, what are some solutions to eating too quickly, skipping meals or eating while you're distracted and in stress mode? Here are four things I often recommend to my patients:

1. Before you start eating, stop and take 10 slow deep breaths in and out. This helps to slow you down, move you into "rest and digest" mode and hopefully helps you to be mindful to eat more slowly and savor your food.

2. Use eating as a time for mindful meditation. Tune in to the tastes, smells and textures of what you're eating. Be aware of how many times you chew your food. Tune in to how fast you're eating. Chances are you need to train yourself to slow down. Take a relaxing breath in and out between mouthfuls. Use this time to be grateful for the (hopefully healthy) food you are eating and how it is helping your body and mind to function well so you can enjoy your life.

3. Take control of your daily schedule. You may be thinking, "How do I do that when I have to get the kids to school, go to work, then take the kids to music lessons and soccer and somehow find time to get food on the table before it starts all over again the next day?" We actually have much more power and control than we think that we do when it comes how we use our time. Make time to eat breakfast, lunch and supper. When you're at work, leave your work station or office during your lunch break and take yourself to a quiet environment to eat.

4. Take time to prepare healthy meals ahead of time so that you're not tempted to grab junk food for you and your family because you're too busy to cook or eat. I'm a huge fan of slow cookers. Company's Coming has some great slow cooker cook books plus some free recipes on their web site. (Please refer to the resources at the end of Chapter 13.)

I hope this chapter has given you some food for thought – pun intended – and helped you to realize that how you eat is just as important as what you eat.

RESOURCES:

1. http://www.webmd.com/diet/can-stress-cause-weight-gain?page=2
2. Leong SL, Madden C, Gray A, Waters D, Horwath C. Faster self-reported speed of eating is related to higher body mass index in a nationwide survey of middle-aged women. *J Am Diet Assoc.* 2011 Aug;111(8):1192-7
3. Goldfield GS, Murray MA, Bucholz A, Henderson K, Obeid N, Kukaswadia A, Flament MF. Family meals and body mass index among adolescent: effects of gender. *Appl Physiol Nutr Metab.* 2011 Aug;36(4):539-46 (Epub 2011 Aug 18)

CHAPTER 29: WHERE, WHEN AND WHY YOU EAT MAY BE CAUSING YOU TO GAIN WEIGHT

In the previous chapter we talked about how the way you eat can impact your digestion and your overall health and well-being. *How* you eat is also directly affected by *where* you eat. I may be dating myself here but remember when kitchen tables were places where we sat to eat and dining rooms were where we had family meals together? Now it seems that the kitchen table is where we place our laptop, mail and newspapers and the dining room just collects dust. Many people get into bad habits of watching TV or reading while eating. Have you ever noticed that when you do this you don't tend to taste your food, let alone chew it properly? Just try relaxing and eating a meal without any distractions and really focus on the tastes and textures of your food. You'll be amazed to see what you've been missing! Plus, your bodymind will love you for taking the time to get into "rest, digest and restore" mode while you're eating. It's important to know that TVs should be in the TV room, not in the bedroom, kitchen or dining room.

The other thing I am seeing more and more in my practice is parents bringing in their children to see me because their children are complaining of "tummy aches", the cause of which their medical doctor has not been able to diagnose. Once I start asking parents if they are teaching their children to sit quietly while they eat, the reason for their children's "tummy aches" becomes readily apparent. Children are being allowed to run around and leave the table to play or watch TV while eating. This, of course, puts them right into "fight or flight" or excitement mode and, as we've already discussed, this is not conducive to having a happy digestive system, let alone a healthy bodymind complex. I cannot emphasize enough the importance of teaching children that they need to be sitting quietly at the table while eating! We have to remember that they are growing and their nervous systems are still developing. If you allow your child to run around and play at meal time you are essentially programming their brains to believe this is normal, healthy behavior when in fact, it is very unhealthy behavior. In other words, it becomes a habit for them and a bad one at that – not to mention the choking hazards. It also means that the "tummy ache" of today will develop into the digestive system pain and illnesses of adolescence and adulthood. Of course if Mom and Dad are running around and modeling unhealthy behavior, it's going to be a challenge to get your child to learn to sit at the table while eating.

Again, at the risk of sounding old fashioned, when I was growing up, we always sat at the table for meals and it was always a time of great conversation, learning and laughter (not that you should talk or laugh with your mouth full!). Of course there were times we had to be quiet while Dad listened to the agriculture reports on the radio, but other than that, meal time was the way it was supposed to be. I realize that in this day and age with both parents working, single parent households and after school activities like soccer, hockey and music lessons, it's even more of a challenge to have family meals. However, if eating at the table is happening more often than eating on the run, everyone will be happier and healthier. A recent Canadian study noted that while "family meals have been identified as a protective factor against obesity among youth", no one had studied to see if there were differences between teenage females and males.[1] Interestingly, this study showed that a higher frequency of family meals, meaning the more often families ate together at home, was associated with a lower body mass index (BMI) for female adolescent family members. A lower BMI means the person is at a healthier weight, a higher BMI is associated with being overweight or obese. They're not sure why this study revealed that having family meals seemed more beneficial to female adolescents than male so further studies are needed. What I find interesting is that a study like this probably would never have been done 25 to 30 years ago because childhood and adolescent obesity were not at the critical levels they are now. Also, it is important to know that there are many factors contributing to being overweight or obese such as stress and emotions. However, as research indicates, being at a healthy weight can start by just sitting down at the table and eating with our families! Even if you're single or an "empty nester", it is still beneficial to sit down at the table at meal times and enjoy your food. Remember, we all have the power to make positive choices for ourselves and our families.

So far we've seen that *how* and *where* you eat impact your overall health. Now let's take a look at how *when* we eat affects us. I'm sure we've all heard that breakfast is the most important meal of the day. If you take a close look at the word breakfast i.e. break fast, it really is breaking the fast. That means eating after the 12 hour (approximately) "fast" you've had from the time you had supper to the time you wake up after eight hours of sleep. In my practice I've heard every excuse in the book why people do not eat breakfast. "Oh, I'm too tired." "I don't have enough time." "I feel nauseas if I eat when I get up." And, the list goes on. If you're too tired to eat breakfast, maybe it's because you're not going to bed early enough or following the basic sleep recommendations I highlighted in Chapter 4. Maybe it's because you're not eating nutritional foods.

Tap out your Cortices or do BodyTalk Access (if you've taken the course) before you even get out of bed. (Refer back to Chapter 2.) I have found this to be particularly helpful if I have to get up earlier than usual. For example, recently I was taking a course and I had to get up at 5:45 am to have breakfast and get ready to go. Usually I get up between 7:00 am and 7:30 am. I used to find it difficult having breakfast earlier than usual as it would slightly upset my stomach. However, now I just tap out my Cortices or do the full BodyTalk Access routine, my stomach feels great and I'm able to enjoy my meal plus get a great start to the day. Another option is to take 10 deep breaths in and out before eating breakfast, or any meal for that matter. If you're too tired to eat breakfast and are relying on caffeine for your energy, you're putting yourself into a dangerous, downward spiral. In fact, you're probably already there. However, it's easy to break the cycle by having breakfast!

An American study looked at the association of the quality and amount of energy or calories found in food adults ate for breakfast and compared that with their BMI.[2] They gathered their information from national surveys done from 1999-2004. The researchers found that women who ate breakfast had a lower BMI compared to women who skipped breakfast. Overall, people who ate breakfast also tended to consume foods with fewer calories the rest of their day compared to people who didn't eat breakfast. However, people who had high calorie breakfasts tended to have a poorer overall diet and higher BMI. So the moral of the story is that it appears that having breakfast is important in maintaining a healthy BMI. However, the *quality* of the food you eat at breakfast is also very important. In other words, let's say you're eating hash browns, greasy sausages and buttermilk pancakes with syrup every day for breakfast. On the one hand, that's great that you're having breakfast. However, for your BMI and overall health, it would be much better if you were having poached eggs on toast instead.

It should be pretty clear by now that our weight and overall health is impacted by *how*, *where* and *when* we eat. Now let's explore some of the key reasons *why* we eat and the effects that can have on us.

Obviously we need to eat to survive. Generally speaking, we can't go more than about three days without water or 30-40 days without food, although there have been some noted exceptions.[3] However, what are some of the other reasons why we eat? Well, we eat to celebrate milestones in our lives. Birthdays, weddings, anniversaries and even funerals are distinguished by the food that plays a key role in these events. Seasonal holidays from Mother's day, summer BBQs, Thanksgiving and Christmas are also times when wonderful food is prepared and shared. Many religious holidays involve preparing special food to eat. Spending quality time with friends and family often takes place over a meal. Romantic dinners are a key part of dating as well as keeping the love alive in established relationships. However, we also often eat when we're stressed, depressed, or lonely, otherwise known as emotional eating. What's important to note is that we need to be aware of *why* we are eating. Whether we're eating because we are happy, sad or just plain hungry because it is mealtime, we need to take note about the quality and the quantity of our food choices. Even overeating healthy food can be bad for us. Also, as I talked about in Chapter 28, eating while distracted, even if it's because you're celebrating something wonderful, can have a negative impact on your digestive system.

I hope this chapter has helped you appreciate the importance of being aware of where, when and why you eat. This awareness can play a key role in making necessary changes that may help you both attain and maintain a healthy weight.

RESOURCES:

1. Goldfield GS, Murray MA, Bucholz A, Henderson K, Obeid N, Kukaswadia A, Flament MF. Family meals and body mass index among adolescents: effects of gender. *Appl Physiol Nutr Metab.* 2011 Aug;36(4):539-46. (Epub 2011 Aug 18)

2. Kant AK, Andon MB, Angelopoulos TJ, Rippe JM. Association of breakfast energy density with diet quality and body mass index in American adults: National Health and Nutrition Examination Surveys, 1999-2004. *Am J Clin Nutrition*, 2008 Nov;88(5):1396-404

Dr. Jennifer Harrison

3. http://www.cbc.ca/news/canada/how-long-can-we-survive-with-out-food-or-water-1.1000898

CHAPTER 30: THREE TIPS FOR KEEPING OFF THE HOLIDAY POUNDS

Over the holidays we're surrounded by lots of wonderful food. It's easy to overeat with all the Christmas parties and meals with friends and family. Also, the holidays can be stressful for a wide variety of reasons. All of this can lend to a tendency toward over-eating. In fact, most people gain five, 10 or even 15 lbs over the holidays. The problem is that we often don't lose all that weight after the holidays are over. So, an ounce of prevention is literally worth a pound of cure. Here are three simple things you can do to help keep from gaining weight during this festive season.

1. Decrease portion sizes by choosing a smaller plate as well as smaller servings. This will help us to decrease the number of calories we're consuming which in turn will help to keep the extra holiday pounds off.

2. Keep to moderate to low alcohol intake. Over the holidays people tend to consume more alcohol than usual at parties and during family get-togethers. Plus, some people use drinking extra alcohol as a way to deal with stress. Aside from the fact that this is an unhealthy way to deal with emotions, there are a few other problems with drinking too much alcohol. One is that most people tend to be dehydrated to start with and alcohol can further dehydrate you, especially your brain. That is what causes hangovers. Secondly, there are a lot of calories in alcoholic beverages. A single large glass of wine, which is considered to be 250mls or one cup of wine, can have almost 230 calories. So, a good strategy is to drink a glass of water after each alcoholic beverage. This will help prevent you from over-drinking. Plus, water will help keep you hydrated and it is calorie free. If you're drinking alcohol because you're stressed or depressed over the holidays, you may want to talk to a counselor or psychologist. They can help you set up strat-

egies or a game plan to deal with difficult family or personal situations. Plus, they'll help you address the core issues so that the
Christmas season is less stressful for you.

3. Be active. A third problem that causes weight gain over the
holidays is that between extra social engagements, travelling to
spend time with family and friends, or having family and friends
come to visit, your exercise routines often go out the window. A
simple way to stay active over the holidays is to go for a walk,
especially after a large meal. It's a nice way to spend time with
your family and friends, plus you're outdoors and getting exercise.
If you happen to live in a part of the world – like Canada – where
sometimes the temperatures plus the wind make it unsafe to walk
outside, stay indoors and play active videos games that involve
moving around. There are lots of options from sports video games
to dance ones. I was visiting friends recently and they have two
little girls. One evening we played a dance video game. Not only
was it hilarious, but after 20 minutes – between the dancing and
the laughing – I was starting to break into a sweat. It's a great
way to stay active and to prevent weight gain. It's also a fun way
to enjoy the holidays and lower your stress.

So, I hope that these three simple strategies will help you keep off
those extra holiday pounds. They're also great ways to help you
Go From Your Stressed Self To Your Best Self™ this Holiday Season.

SECTION 3: EXERCISE

Dr. Jennifer Harrison

CHAPTER 31: DAILY EXERCISE - HOW MUCH DO YOU REALLY NEED?

There's a reason why the TV show *The Biggest Loser* is starting its 16th season and doing a casting call for season 17. People love success stories as well as cheering for the underdog. The ratings for this show are high which, ironically, means a lot of people are sitting on their couches every week watching people get fit, healthy and lose weight. However, how many people are also being inspired to get off their couches to exercise? And, how much exercise do you really need? What type of exercise is right for you? In this chapter I'm going to address these questions and more. You might be surprised by the answers.

In spite of shows like *The Biggest Loser* which resulted in the major career launching of people like Jillian Michaels and Bob Harper, worldwide obesity has doubled since 1980. In spite of the easy access to fitness classes, fitness DVDs, digital downloads and on demand fitness workouts, not to mention free workouts on YouTube, 65 percent of the world's population live in countries where being overweight and obese kills more people than being underweight does. According to the World Health Organization, in 2012, more than 40 million children under the age of five were overweight or obese. Being overweight and obese is 100 percent preventable.[1]

ParticipACTION is a national non-profit organization originally launched by the Canadian Government in the 1970s. According to The Canadian Physical Activity Guidelines, here's how much exercise we should be getting:[2]

"To achieve health benefits, adults aged 18-64 years should accumulate at least 150 minutes of moderate- to vigorous-intensity aerobic physical activity per week, in bouts of 10 minutes or more.

Dr. Jennifer Harrison

It is also beneficial to add muscle- and bone-strengthening activities using major muscle groups, at least two days per week. More physical activity provides greater health benefits.

Some examples [of moderate- to vigorous-intensity exercise] are brisk walking, running, swimming and bicycling. Adults should accumulate this activity over and above the activities of daily living, such as housekeeping, preparing meals and shopping. These guidelines may be appropriate for adults with a disability or medical condition; however, they should consult a health professional to understand the types and amounts of physical activity appropriate for them."

With regard to how to gage whether you're doing moderate to intense physical activity, this is what they say:

"Moderate-intensity physical activities will cause adults to sweat a little and to breathe harder. On a scale of 0 to 10 (with 10 being an absolute maximum effort and 0 being completely at rest), moderate activities are about a 5 or 6. While doing moderate-intensity activity adults should still be able to talk, but not sing along to their favourite song. Vigorous-intensity physical activities will cause adults to sweat and be out of breath. On a scale of 0 to 10 (with 10 being an absolute maximum effort and 0 being completely at rest), vigorous activities are about a 7 or 8. While doing vigorous activity adults shouldn't be able to say more than a few words without pausing for a breath. Adults should do as much vigorous activity as they can."

Interestingly, the Canadian Physical Activity Guidelines for people over age 65 are the same as for the 18 – 64 age group. However, the key difference is that "adults 65 years and older are encouraged to participate in a variety of physical activities that are enjoyable and safe... Those with poor mobility should perform physical activities to enhance balance and prevent falls."

118

Well, what about the kids? The Canadian Physical Activity Guidelines divide children into different age groups.

For children ages 0 – 4, the following is recommended:

"More daily physical activity provides greater benefits. Infants (aged less than 1 year) should be physically active several times daily – particularly through interactive floor-based play. Toddlers (aged 1-2 years) and preschoolers (aged 3-4 years) should accumulate at least 180 minutes of physical activity at any intensity spread throughout the day, including: A variety of activities in different environments, activities that develop movement skills, and progression toward at least 60 minutes of energetic play by 5 years of age."

For children ages 5 – 11, the following guidelines apply:

"For health benefits, children aged 5-11 years should accumulate at least 60 minutes of moderate- to vigorous-intensity physical activity daily. This should include: Vigorous-intensity activities at least 3 days per week and activities that strengthen muscle and bone at least 3 days per week."

The same applies for youth ages 12 – 17.

The Canada Food Guide uses essentially the same recommendations in the Physical Activity section.[3]

It's important to remember that physical activity for children and youth also helps them to develop social skills if they're playing team sports or even just engaging in free play with other children, youth and adults. Exercising as a family is also a great way to spend quality time together plus your children get to see you model a healthy lifestyle. Whether it's going for walks after supper or skiing or swimming, family fit time can also be a fun time. Exercise is very helpful in dealing with stress at any age so getting into the habit at an early age can literally have a lifetime of health benefits.

Dr. Jennifer Harrison

Another great resource is BodyBreak, created by Hal Johnson and Joanne McLeod who were originally involved in starting ParticipACTION and recently competed on the reality show *The Amazing Race*. Be sure to check out their website for great exercise and activity ideas.[4]

Please note that before starting any exercise program, you should check with your medical doctor to make sure you don't have any existing problems which could be made worse with physical activity. It is also a good idea to be checked out by your athletic therapist or sport physiotherapist and chiropractor to make sure you don't have any existing muscle imbalances and joint restrictions which could predispose you to injury if you start working out. They can also recommend which activities would best be suited for you. Plus, if you have an existing or an old nagging injury, get this treated first. You want to set yourself up for success, not failure. This means working with your body, not against it.

In Athletic Therapy we have a saying: "It's better to wear out than to rust out." In other words, regardless of your age, physical ability or current fitness level, get moving and keep moving!

Remember, your fit self is Your Best Self!

RESOURCES:

1. http://www.who.int/mediacentre/factsheets/fs311/en/
2. http://www.participaction.com/
3. http://www.hc-sc.gc.ca/fn-an/food-guide-aliment/basics-base/activit-eng.php
4. http://www.bodybreak.com/

CHAPTER 32: JUNE IS NATIONAL ATHLETIC THERAPY MONTH

I've been a Certified Athletic Therapist for over 25 years and an educator for the Canadian Athletic Therapists Association (CATA) since 2003. However, many people still don't really know what an Athletic Therapist is or know that we are trained to assess and treat anyone who has sustained an activity related injury. So, whether you're a professional athlete, dancer or a mom who injured herself lifting her toddler, a Certified Athletic Therapist can help get you back in your game. In Canada, June is National Athletic Therapy Month and I'd like to share with you the following 2014 press release from the CATA:

National Athletic Therapy Month reminds us that we're all athletes.

While we usually think of sports when we talk about athletic activity, most Canadians engage in some form of physical activity every day. Whether it's lifting an infant into a highchair, running for the bus, or bending to reach a fallen sock behind the dryer, we move and exert our bodies constantly. And sometimes we feel the pain from those movements.

That's the idea behind National Athletic Therapy Month this June: an annual reminder that everyone can benefit from the expertise of Canada's Certified Athletic Therapists. By declaring, "We are all athletes", the Canadian Athletic Therapists Association (CATA) hopes to educate Canadians who have sustained an injury to their muscles, bones, or joints that a Certified Athletic Therapist (CAT(C)) can help get them back to work and play.

"While we're primarily known for our role in helping athletes recover from injury faster and achieve peak performance, our skills can be used to help anyone with an injury," said Richard DeMont,

Dr. Jennifer Harrison

President of CATA. "Whether you're a weekend golfer an avid gardener, or a busy soccer mom, moving without pain or discomfort is an important part of our overall health and well-being."

Being able to translate the knowledge gained from years of treating elite athletes at the highest levels of competitive and professional sports into the needs of all Canadians makes the role of a Certified Athletic Therapist very valuable for injury recovery.

"For professional and elite athletes, the sporting arena is their workplace, and we treat workplace injuries," said DeMont. "Whether that workplace is a playing field or an office tower makes no difference; we help get people back into their game."

From injury prevention to emergency care to rehabilitation, Certified Athletic Therapists are committed to assisting all of life's athletes.

For more information go to the Canadian Athletic Therapists Association web site at: www.athletictherapy.org

CHAPTER 33: GET FIT FOR FREE

With summer time approaching, lots of us are thinking about our beach ready physique – or lack thereof – but really, any time is a great time to get fit and keep fit. However, sometimes our budgets are a bit too tight to accommodate a gym, yoga or Pilates studio membership. Sometimes our schedules just don't permit us to get to that Zumba class. Other times, we're too self-conscious to work out in front of other people. Regardless of your situation, I've got some great news for you on how you can get fit, in the comfort of your own home, for free!

First of all, before you start a fitness program, make sure you've been cleared by your health care professionals. Whether or not you have an existing health issue, like high blood pressure, for example, you should see your medical doctor before you begin exercising. If you're recovering from an injury or have had muscle and/or joint problems in the past, you need to see your athletic therapist or sport physiotherapist and chiropractor to make sure that starting an exercise program won't make things worse. You may need some treatment to help get your body aligned before starting your workouts or you may need some advice on what types of exercise would be best for you and which ones to avoid. Also, they may be able to refer to you a good personal fitness trainer if you need a more individualized workout set up for you.

OK, now that you've been cleared to exercise, here are some great free fitness options that I use and recommend to my patients. I'll also include a great budget conscious option for you.

ExerciseTV on YouTube:

http://www.youtube.com/results?search_query=exercise+tv

ExerciseTV was a US television network that broadcast on digital cable. It had free and video-on-demand options. It was started in 2006 but, unfortunately, went out of business in 2011. The upside

is that many of the workouts led by a variety of top fitness trainers have been uploaded to YouTube. ExerciseTV workouts range
from cardio and abs to yoga, Pilates and personal training. Some
of my favourite fitness trainers include: Kendell Hogan, Amy
Dixon, Jessica Smith (who I'll talk about again in a moment), Vi-
olet Zaki, Stephanie Vitorino, and Teri Ann Krefting. (I personally have fitness DVDs featuring each of them and I love their
workouts!) However, there are literally hundreds of different videos which include 10, 20, 30 and 40 minutes workouts with a huge
variety of trainers. You can do a single workout or combine
workouts. Most of the workouts require light free weights (3 –
10lb dumbbells) and an exercise mat while the cardio workouts
just require that you have a bit of space available in which to
move. This is a great option to have fun and get fit for free in the
comfort of your own home.

Jessica Smith TV on YouTube:

https://www.youtube.com/user/jessicasmithtv

As I mentioned above, Jessica has also uploaded over 200 (and
counting) free fitness videos to YouTube that cover a variety of
workouts. She adds new ones every week. On her web site she has
them currently organized under a variety of categories such as
beginner, knee and back friendly, Pilates and yoga inspired, Abs,
Cardio, and much more. Again, this is a great way to get fit for
free! Her website also promotes her professional fitness DVDs and
video downloads that you can purchase from her web site or from
online stores. Jessica gives really good instruction, is upbeat and
down to earth.

The Caribbean Workout: Another one of my faves is the TV show
The Caribbean Workout led by Canadian fitness expert, Shelly
McDonald. The show went from 1994 to 2011. As of the writing of
this book, I couldn't find it being aired on any Canadian or US
stations anymore. However, you can find some episodes that have

been uploaded to YouTube. If you want to make a purchase, you can download the complete first season (24 episodes) featuring Shelly on iTunes. The episodes include yoga and Pilates inspired workouts as well as Boot camp style and on the go workouts you can do when you are travelling and don't have access to a gym.

GaiamTV: Healthy living company Gaiam provides the fourth option I want to share with you. They've also created GaiamTV. They call it the "Transformation Network" and there are currently five "channels" including: my yoga, health and longevity, seeking truth, spiritual growth, films and series. You can sign up for a free 10-day trial and, if you like it, join for a monthly or annual fee. In addition to yoga workouts, if you click on "Fitness" under "My Yoga" you'll find a variety of fitness videos available to view. I haven't personally tried GaiamTV. However, many of the fitness videos come from DVDs that I already own. Some of my favourite fitness trainers featured there are: Ana Caban (Pilates expert – I own all of her Pilates videos and they're amazing!), Tanja Djelevic (I have more than half a dozen of her workouts which include using the balance disc, stability ball, weighted exercise ball, resistance cord or just your own body weight. They're great!), Suzanne Deason who is a yoga and Pilates expert, Madeleine Lewis, and many more. They also have workouts from The Firm, an American fitness company who has been producing fitness videos for well over 20 years. I have lots of their DVDs, too, and have found them to be good workouts featuring different instructors. They always have a beginner modifying the workouts so, if you're just starting out, it's pretty easy to follow. On GaiamTV there are free video clips so you can get a feel for the workout and the instructor.

Never underestimate the benefits of walking! Whether you like to walk outside, go to your local shopping mall and do laps or take a stroll on your treadmill while you watch your favourite TV show or movie, walking is a great form of exercise. It's easily accessible and it's free! Remember, everything counts. Even if you do 3 ten minute walking segments during your day, that still has the same health benefits as if you'd walked for 30 minutes straight.

So, whether you are looking to get bikini ready or you just want to get fit, healthy and strong, here are five great options (including free and budget conscious ones) to help you on your way. And remember, always work with your body, not against it!

Your fit self is Your Best Self!

Please Note: I am not affiliated with any of the programs or products I have mentioned in this article and do not receive compensation, financial or otherwise, from these people or companies. They are simply products and programs that I have found to be very beneficial and I wanted to share them with you.

CHAPTER 34: THE OLYMPICS - WHAT'S IN IT FOR US?

Author's Note: I wrote this article in February, 2014, just before the start of the Sochi Winter Olympics. While those Olympics have come and gone, I feel the points in this article can apply to us for wherever we may be on our life journey.

Well, the XXII Winter Olympics in Sochi, Russia, will soon be starting. More than 2500 athletes from 88 countries around the world will be competing in 98 events in 15 different sports disciplines. This will be followed by the XI Paralympics in which athletes will be competing in 72 events in six sports with para-snowboarding being featured for the first time in Paralympic history.[1] While there is much excitement building, we're also aware of the many controversies surrounding the games including historical, environmental and economic issues plus the safety and human rights of lesbian, gay, bisexual and transgender (LGBT) athletes, supporters and journalists. All the excitement and the controversy have me asking some questions like:

1. What can we learn from watching men and women who have devoted literally years, and in some cases decades, of their lives to being their "Best Self" in a sport?

2. How can our bodymind health benefit from watching the Winter Olympics/Paralympics?

3. What can we learn from the pre-Olympic/Paralympic controversies?

4. What's in it for us?

What can we learn from watching the Olympics? I've noticed in the past couple of Olympics, summer and winter, that the media have been focusing a lot on the human aspect of the athletes. They've had special clips of interviews with many of the athletes

Dr. Jennifer Harrison

helping us get to know them as people as well as athletes. The media has allowed them to share their struggles and their victories with us. I always find this inspiring. It's easy to look at Olympic athletes as somehow being "super humans" and that their lives are simpler than ours because all they have to do is train and compete and everything else in their lives is taken care of. Of course, in many cases this couldn't be further from the truth.

Take Canadian Olympic downhill skier Larisa Yurkiw.[2] After being sidelined from her sport for almost two years with a devastating knee injury (she tore two ligaments, one tendon and both menisci which are special pieces of cartilage in the knee joint), when she did finally come back, Alpine Canada cut her from the National Team, even though she was the reigning national downhill champion. This meant that all her funding was cut, too. Instead of just calling it quits, she rallied and managed, on her own and with the help of family, friends and corporate sponsors, to raise the tens of thousands of dollars needed to hire a coach, pay for equipment, travel, food, physiotherapy rehab, etc. so she could compete on the World Cup circuit. In addition to that, she has skied so well this season that she earned a place on the Canadian Olympic Ski Team! She has shown what is possible and how to Go From Your Stressed Self To Your Best Self™.

In my opinion, every single Paralympian is an inspiration! They all have amazing stories, many of them involving how life threatening accidents caused them to become disabled in some way. But, somehow, they were able to overcome that and become some of the best athletes in the world!

Another interesting story is that of Prince Alfonso von Hohenlohe. Although he is competing for Mexico in skiing, he's only one eighth Mexican and he's actually a royal descendent from a German principality that hasn't existed for over 200 years! The other thing that is even more amazing is that he will be the second-oldest winter Olympian at the Sochi games at age 55! That means

128

he'll be competing against skiers who are more than half his age! How inspiring is that?

And let's not forget Team Canada flag bearer Hayley Wickenheiser. In addition to being a member of the Canadian women's national ice hockey team for the past 20 years (since she was 15), she was also the first woman to play full-time professional hockey in a position other than goalie. She has represented Canada at the Winter Olympics four times, capturing three gold medals and one silver and twice being named tournament MVP, as well as one time at the Summer Olympics in softball. In addition to widely being considered the greatest female ice hockey player in the world, she's also a mom, plus this will be her fifth Winter Olympics – sixth overall! Another example of how passion and persistence pays off.

How can our bodymind health benefit from watching the Olympics? We get to watch all these very fit and healthy athletes. I think the Olympics are a great motivator to get us to either start an exercise program, resume a lapsed one or take our current workouts to the next level. Even though we may be sitting on the couch watching the Olympics on TV, that doesn't mean that we can't be inspired to get moving more. Plus, you know that these athletes are eating their fruits and veggies and lean protein. With childhood and adult obesity continuing to be on the rise, we can all benefit from some Olympic motivation!

Another thing to recognize from a bodymind perspective is that Olympic athletes don't "just happen" – they are created out of goal setting, taking action and having the support of their families, friends, communities, coaches, sports psychologists, athletic therapists, sport physios, massage therapists, chiropractors, sports medicine doctors, orthopaedic surgeons as well as provincial and national sporting bodies. No one is an island. It's nice to see the media highlight some of these behind the scenes people to help us realize that even in individual sports, it's a team effort! Skier Larisa Yurkiw is a great example of this. It is also a good reminder of how important it is to create our own supportive team to help us in our own lives.

So, what can we learn from the pre-Olympic/Paralympic controversies? I must say it's been pretty disconcerting to read about the human rights violations taking place in Russia, not to mention the environmental and economic issues. Also, I learned that there is a group of Circassian nationalists who demand the events be cancelled or moved unless Russia apologizes for deaths that occurred in the 19th-century, which Circassians consider genocide. This was a piece of history of which I was not previously aware. Can these controversies be overcome? I would say definitely yes! The reason I say this is that the Olympics repeatedly show us that countries, some of whom have extreme political differences, can compete peacefully against one another. More than that, athletes from different countries actually become friends! It shows what is possible when our focus is on excellence and respect, regardless of nationality, the historical past, sexuality and gender. Mother Teresa said the answer to creating world peace is to go home and love your family. With the Olympics, sometimes your "family" becomes an entire National Team with some inspirational "long lost relatives" from other countries!

So, with regard to the Sochi Winter Olympics, what's really in it for us? Well, I would say the following:

Inspiration to tackle life's challenges.

Motivation to exercise more and eat healthier.

Recognition of the importance of goal setting and building a supportive team to help us through our rough times as well as in achieving our life goals.

Seeing that it is possible to set aside politics and have countries compete peacefully against one another.

Here's to all of us focusing on being our Best Self!

RESOURCES:

1. http://en.wikipedia.org/wiki/2014_Winter_Olympics
2. http://www.escarpmentmagazine.ca/flipzine/2013-winter/files/assets/basic-html/page14.html
3. http://ca.eonline.com/news/504102/meet-one-of-the-most-interesting-athletes-competing-in-the-2014-winter-olympics

Dr. Jennifer Harrison

CHAPTER 35: HOW TO HAVE A SUMMER VACATION EVERY DAY

With the economy and job security being uncertain, many people will not be able to afford the cost of a summer vacation. In 2014, according to a BMO Financial survey, nearly a quarter (22 percent) were planning more staycations that year and more than half intended to vacation strictly within their home province. According to Travelocity.ca, in 2013, 83 percent of Canadians did not travel on any given long weekend and the majority say they regret it. Sounds like doom and gloom, right?

If you stop and think about it, why do we take vacations? It's either to de-stress or to explore new places. Sometimes it's a combination of the two. Regardless, taking time to relax and have fun isn't just a frivolous notion. It's actually essential for good bodymind health! So, whether you are planning on taking a week or just going away for a weekend, there is also a way that you can have a summer vacation every day!

According to a Scientific American Mind article, research shows that there are four key ingredients to maximizing the mental boost you need from a vacation.[1]

1. Rural is restorative: People find that being out in the country is the best choice for decreasing stress and enhancing their mood.

2. Be active: People who spent more time engaging in physical activity on a winter vacation or weekend getaway reported significantly greater satisfaction. I'm sure this applies to a summer vacation, too.

3. Even a weekend vacation can do the trick: The aftereffects may not last long, but research shows that an impromptu short vacation can improve psychological well-being in the moment.

Dr. Jennifer Harrison

4. Planning is half the fun: Some studies show that people get the most vacation-related pleasure from organizing their trip. So if money is tight, try planning a staycation. Mapping out fun new things to do in your hometown or region may deliver a similar jolt of happiness.

I'd like to add a few of my own recommendations to help you max-imize your vacation time and even to help you make every day (or at least a part of it) a vacation.

1. Tap out your Cortices: Refer back to "Chapter 2: Decrease Your Stress in Under 90 Seconds with the Cortices Technique" if you need to remind yourself how to use this great de-stressing tool.

2. Take time every day to be outside, preferably in nature: If you live in a town or city, this could mean your backyard, taking a walk around the block or going to a city park.

3. Take time to meditate: Lots of my patients tell me that they can't meditate. Their minds just won't shut off. What's important to realize is that there are many different kinds of meditation. (Refer to "Chapter 1: Meditation: Which Type is Right for You?") While extremely effective, transcendental meditation (which in-volves clearing the mind of thought) can be a bit of a daunting place to start if you're just learning to meditate. Many people find guided meditations easier to do. There are lots of audio CDs, iTunes recordings, podcasts or app downloads that you can use. On iTunes, many of the recordings or podcasts are free so you can get a feel for what guided meditation is like. If you go on YouTube and search for "guided meditation", you'll get over 800,000 op-tions! Meditation is a simple yet powerful way to give your mind and body a vacation every day. It can also enhance your actual vacation by helping you get into relaxation mode more quickly so that you spend less time unwinding from your hectic life and more time in actual holiday mode.

134

4. Consider taking a staycation: As much as I like to travel, I'm also a fan of the staycation. Part of that could be because I live in Calgary, Alberta, and with the Canadian Rockies less than 90 minutes away, there are many amazing places to see and things to do right in my own backyard. If you are doing a staycation, be intentional about creating a "vacation mindset". What I mean by this is don't let yourself get into the "I'm home so I should get caught up on…" mode. If you really do have things that need doing, set aside a day or maybe two of your time off to complete them. Then, make each day a vacation day and let yourself relax, guilt free!

5. Make time to play! Play with your kids, your dog and your friends. Playing games outside like beach volleyball or lawn games like bocce ball are lots of fun and get you outdoors. If it's a rainy day, there are tons of board or active video games that can help boost your endorphins (happy hormones) so that you really enjoy your vacation time, wherever you may be.

So whether you take a vacation or a staycation, remember, your holiday self is Your Best Self!

RESOURCES:

1. http://www.scientificamerican.com/article/4-ways-to-plan-a-mind-restoring-vacation/

Dr. Jennifer Harrison

CHAPTER 36: SLIPPING INTO SEPTEMBER

Well, it's after Labour Day Weekend and we've all been thrown into the craziness known as September. One of the things I see in my practice every year is that people have either been really active over the summer – biking, hiking, swimming, etc. – or they've been lounging in their backyard, by the pool or at the edge of the lake all summer. Either way, it seems in the busyness of back to work, back to school or back to fall and winter extracurricular commitments, one of the things to go by the wayside is regular physical activity. Before you sign up for the yoga, Zumba or boot camp class, there are some really important things you need to know.

Firstly, always check with your medical doctor as well as an athletic therapist or sport physiotherapist and your chiropractor before starting an exercise routine. The reason for seeing your medical doctor is to make sure that exercising is not going to harm you or adversely affect your health. For example, you may have high blood pressure and not know it. While regular exercise can help with that, it could also cause you to have a heart attack or stroke if the underlying cause of the high blood pressure isn't diagnosed and addressed first.

The reason for seeing your athletic therapist or sport physio and chiropractor is to make sure that any underlying muscle and joint imbalances or restrictions can be treated. Also, these health care practitioners can help you decide which type of exercise is going to be best for your body. For example, if you've been a couch potato for the past 10 years, jumping into a boot camp class may not be your best choice and may actually cause you to injure yourself. Similarly, certain low back conditions will respond really well to yoga and Pilates, while other back conditions can be made worse. Athletic therapists, sport physios and chiropractors can help you with that. Also, by identifying any underlying muscle and joint imbalances, athletic therapists and sport physios in particular,

137

Dr. Jennifer Harrison

can help design a specific workout program for you to help restore proper muscle and joint balance, thus decreasing your risk of injury.

Secondly, work with your body not against your body. I'm always telling my patients this. We've all heard the old adage "no pain, no gain". However, people usually take it out of context. This old saying actually means that you will have to push yourself out of your comfort zone if you are going to increase your cardiovascular endurance, muscle strength and flexibility. If you feel actual pain, this is your body's way of letting you know that something is wrong and you need to stop what you are doing immediately. Always, with no exceptions! Then, it's usually good to follow up with your health care practitioner to "find the cause and treat the cause" of the pain.

Thirdly, if you're used to being physically active but got out of your routine over the summer, be sure to ease your way back into your workouts. A common way that people get injured is by doing too much, too soon. If you've been away from your workout routine for a couple of months, I always recommend decreasing your weights and cardiovascular activity by half for the first week to give your body a chance to get back into the swing of things. Then, gradually over the next few weeks, build yourself back up to where you left off.

Once you've got the workout routine that is right for you, stick with it. You'll feel happier and be healthier!

CHAPTER 37: IS YOUR FITBIT HARMING YOUR HEALTH?

What do Fitbit, Jawbone, Misfit and Striiv have in common? These pieces of "wearable technology" all use wireless radio frequencies to both transmit and receive information. Although it seems like wireless devices have been overtaking our daily lives more and more in the past few years, wireless technology has actually been around since the late 1800s. In 1878, David Hughes was able to transmit a radio signal over a few hundred feet using a special device. In 1880, Alexander Graham Bell and Charles Sumner Tainter invented and patented the photophone and had the first wireless phone conversation. While the fitness technology that you wear or the nutrition and fitness apps you use on your cell phone can be very useful in helping you achieve your health and fitness goals, what most people don't realize is that there are potential health hazards from excessive exposure to certain frequencies of radio waves. Did you know that your cell phone, tablet and other wireless devices, including baby monitors, come with warnings? In this article I want to help raise your awareness about the possible health hazards related to using wireless technology. I also want to offer some concrete suggestions on how you can minimize the risk for yourself and your family while still taking advantage of some of the benefits wireless devices have to offer.

Concerns about electromagnetic field pollution have been around for decades. Dr. Robert O. Becker, a medical doctor, wrote a book in 1990 called *Cross Currents: The Perils of Electromagnetic Pollution, The Promise of Electromedicine*. In the book he talked about the promise of using electromedicine to help with healing but he also warned "that our bodies are being adversely affected by power lines, computers, microwaves and satellite dishes."[1] This was well before the onslaught of cell phone use.

Dr. Jennifer Harrison

According to the World Health Organization (WHO), in 2014 there was an estimated 6.9 billion cell phone subscriptions around the world.[2] This number, of course, continues to grow. In 1996, the WHO established the International Electromagnetic Fields (EMF) Project to look at the scientific evidence of possible adverse health effects from electromagnetic fields. To date, the research that has been evaluated has been inconclusive, meaning that some research has shown apparent links between cell phone use and head and neck cancer while others have not. However, the research has prompted the International Agency for Research on Cancer (IARC) to classify electromagnetic fields as possibly carcinogenic (cancer causing) to humans.[2] The challenge with this research is that the negative effects of certain EMFs may take many decades to become apparent. It's similar to cigarettes. The awareness of the hazards of cigarette smoking, not to mention the risks of inhaling second hand smoke, came many decades after smoking became prevalent in society.

The other thing to note is that it's not just cancer that is a concern. Some research has indicated that exposure to cell phone radiation can cause a decrease in sperm quality in men. This isn't necessarily linked with infertility but researcher Fiona Matthews, PhD, did have this to say. "I would not argue that use of a phone is going to suddenly make men infertile...However, given the increasing use of wireless devices, and general declines in sperm quality seen over the last 10-20 years across the developed world, this is certainly an area that is in urgent need of research."[3] Jamie Griffo, another researcher and medical doctor recommended, "Don't ditch your cell phone, but be smart in how you use it -- don't put your cell phone in your front pocket."[3]

What about the risk to children? L. Lloyd Morgan, a senior scientist along with his colleagues at Environmental Health Trust, did a review of various research and their findings were published in 2014. The review, which was discussed in the August 13, 2014,

140

MedScape article Children Face the Highest Health Risk From Cell Phones, showed that "children and unborn babies face the highest risk for neurologic and biologic damage that results from MWR (microwave radiation) emitted by wireless devices...The rate of absorption is higher in children than adults because their brain tissues are more absorbent, their skulls are thinner, and their relative size is smaller. The fetus is particularly vulnerable because MWR exposure can result in degeneration of the protective myelin sheath that surrounds brain neurons...Multiple studies have shown that children absorb more MWR than adults. One found that the brain tissue of children absorbed about 2 times more MWR than that of adults (*Phys Med Biol.* 2008;53:3681-3695), and other studies have reported that the bone marrow of children absorbs 10 times more MWR than that of adults."[4] Dr. L. Dade Lunsford, who is a medical doctor and researcher at the University of Pittsburgh and not associated with the above mentioned research, shared that while he thought that the warnings coming from the study were appropriate, there were issues with some of the data and some reports were anecdotal.[4]

So, what do we do with all this information? How do we make sense of all this research which seems to be not only controversial but also contradictory? Well, here are some practical actions that we can all take[5, 6]:

1. Hold your cell phone 15cm (six inches) away from your ear as this will provide a 10,000-fold decrease in risk. For laptop computers and tablets, the minimum distance should be 20 cm (about eight inches) from the body.[6] Yes, 20 cm! So really, a laptop computer shouldn't actually be on your lap at all!

2. Any wireless device, unless it is turned off, is always emitting microwave radiation. Therefore, when you're not using your cell phone or tablet, it should not be kept on the body. You should keep it in your purse, bag or backpack. This is what concerns me about

Fitbit and other "wearable technology" because people are wearing them 24/7. These fitness devices can also monitor the quality of your sleep so some people never take them off.

3. Wireless devices should be kept away from the abdomens of pregnant women and should not be used while nursing an infant.

4. Wireless baby monitors should not be placed in an infant's crib. In fact, it's recommended that people should use a baby monitor that is plugged into the wall (non-wireless) so that transmitting radio waves are eliminated.

5. Cell phones should not be allowed in children's bedrooms at night. "The Pew Research Center has reported that 75 percent of preteens and early teens sleep all night with their cell phone under their pillow."[5] This is a very unhealthy habit to get into.

6. Boys and men should not keep a cell phone in their front pockets because of the research I mentioned above suggesting that chronic exposure to radio waves from wireless devices affect the quality of sperm.

7. Girls and women should not keep cells phones in their bras. This recommendation is based on a case study of four young women who developed breast cancer, two at the age of 21. While this is not a conclusive study, it's worth taking the precaution.

8. Because more radiation is absorbed with more hours of using wireless devices such as cell phones and tablets, children should be taught to use these devices as little as possible. Using a landline and having your laptop plugged into the internet instead of using a wireless connection is preferable.

9. Wi-fi routers at home should be placed away from where both adults and children spend a lot of time.

10. I would add that you only use your Fitbit, Jawbone or other wireless fitness technology, including apps on your cell phone,

when you're exercising and definitely remove it and turn it off when not in use.

It is interesting to note that countries such as Belgium, France, India and others where wireless technology is widely used, are passing laws and/or issuing warnings about how children use wireless devices. In Canada in January, 2015, Conservative MP, Terence Young, proposed a non-partisan private Bill C-648 calling for warning labels (which are put in manuals that come with wireless devices but which the majority of people never read) to be "posted prominently on either the device's box or on the device itself....The World Health Organization places wireless radiation on the same cancer warning-list as DDT, lead and car exhaust," Young said at an announcement on Monday. "Canadians have a right to know this."[6]

I hope you've found this information helpful. Wireless technology is not going away and indeed provides many advantages in our day to day lives. However, that doesn't mean that we can't all be more aware and more careful about how we use it. Healthy self is your Best Self!

RESOURCES:

1. Becker, Robert O. *Cross Currents: The Perils of Electropollution, The Promise of Electromedicine*, New York: Jeremy P. Tarcher/Penguin, 1990.
2. http://www.who.int/mediacentre/factsheets/fs193/en/
3. http://www.huffingtonpost.com/2014/06/12/mobile-phone-sperm_n_5486067.html
4. http://www.medscape.com/viewarticle/829881
5. http://www.webmd.com/children/news/20140819/children-cell-phones?page=2
6. https://ca.news.yahoo.com/blogs/dailybrew/does-canada-need-health-warning-labels-on-192334438.html

Dr. Jennifer Harrison

7. http://citizensforsafetechnology.org/Warning-Labels-for-cell-phones-and-WiFi-Bill-C648-to-protect-Canadians-from-radiation,15,4122
8. http://www.c4st.org/PMB

SECTION 4: RELATIONSHIPS

Dr. Jennifer Harrison

CHAPTER 38: HOW FALLING IN LOVE AFFECTS US RIGHT DOWN TO OUR DNA

With February being Heart Month, how can we not think about love? Whether you're falling in love, falling out of love, looking for love or continuing to celebrate years of love with your soul mate, your body can experience a variety of physical sensations. However, let's take a look at some fascinating things that can happen to your body and mind when you're falling in love. The Huffington Post printed an interesting article recently[1] and I want to share the highlights with you, plus some of my own!

Scientists study weird and wonderful things, including what happens to us when we're in love. Research shows that when you are hit with Cupid's arrow the following can happen:

1. Love makes you "dumb". Studies have shown that people who are madly in love are less able to stay focused and have trouble performing tasks that require attention. Of course, you are focused, it's just that you're thinking of your loved one, not on the task at hand.

2. Love makes you high. MRI scans have shown that the same portion of the brain associated with cocaine addiction lights up when you're in love. Reminds me of the '80s song by Roxy Music called "Love is the Drug".

3. Love can take away the pain. Again, it appears that some areas of the brain that get activated by feelings of intense love are the same areas affected by drugs designed to decrease pain. Even holding hands or looking at a photo of a loved one was shown to alleviate pain in female patients.

4. Love makes you walk slower. Well, for men, anyway. Research has shown that men will slow down their walking speed to match that of their beloved, but not when walking with someone they consider just a friend.

147

5. Love changes your heartbeats. Some studies suggest that when you're in love, your heart rate tends to change to match that of your partner. One study showed that this tended to happen with women more than men, but they weren't sure why.

6. Love makes your voice goes higher. Women tend to speak in higher tones to men to whom they're attracted. However, research also showed that both men and women who are in love alter their voices when speaking to each other.

7. Love makes you blind. Some studies show that people in committed relationships who have just been thinking about their beloved will actually unknowingly avoid looking at attractive people in what scientists call "unconscious attentional bias".

8. Love turns you into a daredevil. Some research shows that men are more willing to take unnecessary risks for a romantic partner.

9. Love makes your pupils enlarge. Googly-eyed isn't exactly a scientific term but when you're in love, your pupils will be dilated. Of course pupils also change in size when we're stressed or trying to do complicated math. However, the next time you're gazing into the eyes of your special someone, check out their pupils.

10. Love changes DNA. Research done by the Institute of Heart-Math showed that "… when individuals are in a heart-focused, loving state and in a more coherent mode of physiological functioning, they have a greater ability to alter the conformation (shape or structure) of DNA."[2]

I'm not sure if love can move mountains, but the research shows that our minds and bodies are definitely altered by this powerful and life changing thing called love.

RESOURCES:

1. http://www.huffingtonpost.com/2013/12/02/falling-in-love-strange-things_n_4340958.html?ncid=edlin-kusaolp00000003&ir=Healthy%20Living
2. http://www.heartmath.org/templates/ihm/e-newsletter/publi-cation/2012/winter/emotions-can-change-your-dna.php

Dr. Jennifer Harrison

CHAPTER 39: THE KEY TO A HEALTHY HEART - WHAT MOST DOCTORS DON'T KNOW

February is Heart Month as promoted by the Canadian Heart and Stroke Foundation. We all know that stopping smoking and limiting alcohol and caffeine intake are very important factors in attaining and maintaining good heart health. But what is the real key to a healthy heart? If you said eating well, exercising regularly and managing stress, you wouldn't be wrong. These are also significant factors to having a healthy cardiovascular system. However, there is something else, something so basic and yet essential to heart health and indeed, our very survival. Something that most doctors and health care professionals aren't even aware of. What is this critical element that literally every person on the planet needs?

Dr. Dean Ornish in an American cardiologist who was ridiculed for years when he performed research and later published his book showing that coronary artery disease could actually be reversed through making lifestyle changes. In his 1990 book, *Dr. Dean Ornish's Program for Reversing Heart Disease Without Drugs or Surgery*, he outlined how people could actually change the physical state of their diseased hearts by making dietary changes, exercising more and quitting smoking. However, more than that, he also talked about the importance of "opening your heart to your feelings and to inner peace"[1] which is actually the title of one of the chapters in his book. He talks about yoga and meditation as means to decrease stress. While there is no question that this is beneficial to our health on many levels, there was something else that he discovered that was even more crucial to a healthy heart: love and intimacy!

In his book, *Love and Survival: The Scientific Basis for the Healing Power of Intimacy*, Dr. Ornish says that "When you feel loved, nurtured, cared for, supported, and intimate, you are much more

151

Dr. Jennifer Harrison

likely to be happier and healthier. You have a much lower risk of getting sick and, if you do, a much greater chance of surviving."[2] He demonstrates that when we don't have love and intimacy or healthy versions of it, this at the root of what makes us sick, sad and suffer. However, he also shows that love and intimacy are also what makes us well and bring happiness and healing. "If a new drug had the same impact, virtually every doctor in the country would be recommending it for their patients." (From the publisher on the dust cover.)

Are you feeling loved, nurtured and cared for? Do you have supportive and intimate relationships in your life? While technology no doubts connects us with people literally around the globe through email, Skype, Facebook and Twitter, are we really connecting with our hearts? Do we consciously create relationships in our lives that are supportive and nurturing to us? By creating intimate relationships, not only are they going to be supportive for us, but, by their very nature, they will be mutually beneficial. This is the foundation of healthy and flourishing relationships, families, communities, work places, organizations, cities and beyond. Do you tell your partner, children and friends that you love them? When was the last time you looked in the mirror and said, "I love you!"?

I highly recommend reading Dr. Ornish's books. A chiropractic classmate gave me *Love and Survival* as a thank you gift when she came and stayed with us for a few weeks after graduation. It has proven to be a very valuable gift and this chapter has inspired me to re-read it!

RESOURCES:

1. Ornish, Dean. *Dr. Dean Ornish's Program for Reversing Heart Disease. The Only System Scientifically Proven to Reverse Heart Disease Without Drugs or Surgery.* New York: Ballentine Books, 1990.

2. Ornish, Dean, *Love and Survival. The Scientific Basis for the Healing Power of Intimacy.* New York: HarperCollins Publishers, 1998. p. 24.

Dr. Jennifer Harrison

CHAPTER 40: WHO DO WE LOVE?

I'm a huge fan of the TV show *The Big Bang Theory*. For followers of the show, you know that Sheldon drives Penny crazy with his obsessive three part knocking on her door: knock, knock, knock, "Penny", knock, knock, knock, "Penny", knock, knock, knock, "Penny". So in one episode, Penny teases Sheldon by saying "Who do we love?" as he's knocking so it goes, "Who do we love?", "Penny", "Who do we love?", "Penny", "Who do we love?", "Penny". Then she opens the door with a big smile on her face, much to Sheldon's annoyance.

All joking aside, who do we love? It's easy to come up with a list of people we don't like and who drive us crazy. It may be co-workers, family members or an ex-spouse or partner. Ironically, the people we do love are often the ones we take for granted. However, what I would like to explore in this chapter is the one key person we usually don't love enough and they're involved in every single relationship we have!

What's the common denominator in all of your relationships, the good ones and the not so good ones? YOU! One of the most important relationships we have is with ourselves. If you're not happy with you and you don't like yourself very much let alone love yourself, how can you expect to be in happy and positive relationships with others? Whether it's family, friends, co-workers, your spouse or partner, neighbours or clients, how you feel about yourself will be reflected in the interactions you have with the people in your life. I'm not talking about conceit or narcissism. These are not aspects of true self love. I'm talking about being able to look at yourself in the mirror, smile and say "I love you." I'm talking about being happy with who you are, "faults and all". I'm talking about healthy self-esteem or love of self. Psychotherapist Dr. Nathanial Branden, an expert on self-esteem, believes that "How we feel about ourselves crucially affects virtually every aspect of our experience, from the way we function at work, in

Dr. Jennifer Harrison

love, in sex, to the way we operate as parents, to how high in life we are likely to rise…I cannot think of a single psychological problem that is not traceable to a poor self-concept. Positive self-esteem is a cardinal requirement of a fulfilling life."[1] Researcher and vulnerability expert Dr. Brené Brown says that learning to love ourselves and others requires empathy and compassion. Positive self-worth gives "purpose and meaning to life."[2]

Not sure where to start with this? Well, first, take a look at the people who push your buttons. The ones who tend to tick you off. What's a common theme in your interactions with these people? What do you think is the root cause? What life lesson can you learn from these situations? Sometimes people who really irritate us are actually just mirroring back to us an aspect of ourselves that we really don't like. While there are many great self-help and self-development books out there, I've found the BodyTalk System to be very helpful in my self-discovery journey.[3] If the problem is more complicated or you really don't know where to start, you may want to seek out the advice of a counselor or psychologist to help you on your journey toward having a healthier relationship with yourself.

The second part is to look at the people you love in your life. Who do you love? Is the relationship balanced, meaning are your feelings of love and respect reciprocated? How do you feel when you think about the people you love? When I say "love", I mean all types of love including romantic love, familial love, deep friendship love and spiritual love. This could even include the love you have for your pet. The power of love to heal has been demonstrated in interesting research. For example, in his book, *Love and Survival: The Scientific Basis for the Healing Power of Intimacy*, cardiologist Dr. Dean Ornish talks about what he has found to be "the most powerful and meaningful intervention" for coronary artery disease and that "is love and intimacy and the emotional and spiritual transformation that often results."[4]

156

So, I invite you to focus, even meditate on love and work on nurturing the loving relationships you have in your life, and most importantly, work on loving yourself!

RESOURCES:

1. Branden, Nathanial. *How to Raise Your Self-Esteem: The Proven, Action-Oriented Approach to Greater Self-Respect and Self-Confidence.* New York: Bantam Books, 1987.
2. http://brenebrown.com/
3. www.bodytalksystem.com
4. Ornish, Dean. *Love and Survival: The Scientific Basis for the Healing Power of Intimacy.* New York: HarperCollins Publishers, 1998.

Dr. Jennifer Harrison

CHAPTER 41: GRIEF - THE FINAL FRONTIER

"Space: the final frontier". This classic opening line to the TV series *Star Trek* is known the world over. Well, just the way space may be the final frontier, I think that in our culture, grief is the final frontier. In this chapter, I want to share some ideas I have about grief and grieving as well as some ways we can all live more authentically and compassionately with ourselves and others.

Have you ever noticed that it has become acceptable for basically anyone, whether they be a Hollywood celebrity or someone on *Dr. Phil*, to go on TV, the internet or to write a book and talk about their childhood abuse, their addictions ranging from drugs and alcohol to sex, their eating disorders or infidelities? It may even be profitable to confess to the public to a crime they have committed. An example is the TV show *Orange is the New Black* based on the autobiographical book by the same name.

Now don't get me wrong. In many cases, I think it has been extremely helpful to get some of these topics out into the open for discussion after years of keeping them behind closed doors. However, the point I'm trying to make is that no one talks about grief.

With regard to grief, I think it's really important to recognize that grief isn't just something we feel after a loved one has passed on. There are many things that can cause us to experience grief or a deep sense of loss: losing our job, having a boss or co-worker leave, having a close friend move away, the ending of a relationship, a change in family dynamics, going through a divorce, having a miscarriage, being forced to change jobs or have the company we work for taken over by another, moving to a new city or neighbourhood, children growing up and moving away from home, having a serious health issue affect us or a loved one, watching our parents age (which can trigger anticipatory grief or the anticipation of a loss) and even the loss of a pet. All of these things can cause us to grieve. Grief involves mourning the loss of the familiar whether

159

that be a person, a place or even objects. I have had patients experience grief as they aged and started losing the ability to do things they used to enjoy and losing their independence.

I feel there are some critical steps that may be helpful when dealing with grief.

Naming It: Over the years, I've had many patients and friends not even recognize that what they were experiencing was grief. Any type of perceived loss (like the ones I named above) can trigger the emotions of grief and sadness. If you're feeling "out of sorts" after going through one or more of the grief causing events I listed above, you're probably experiencing grief.

Feeling It: The emotion of grief will be experienced differently by each person depending on how they were taught by their parents and family, based on their religious and spiritual beliefs as well as cultural beliefs, including North American culture. Beyond sadness and crying, you may experience grief by feeling tired or even exhausted. I remember when I did a grief and bereavement course after my Mom died, we were told that when you're grieving, it takes up about 80 percent of your energy which leaves you with 20 percent of your energy to do what normally would take up 100 percent of your energy (working, looking after your kids, volunteer work, exercising, etc.). I also experienced stomach and abdominal pain for a couple of months after my Mom passed which was highly unusual for me as I'd always had a healthy digestive system. I ended up seeing a friend of mine who was a Reiki Master. After her treatment session with me which, by the way, got rid of the stomach pain I'd been experiencing for weeks, she told me that my heart was so full of pain it couldn't process it all so some of the emotional pain had been sent energetically to my stomach. Later on that same year was when I experienced The BodyTalk System for the first time and started my training which further helped with my grief. Now all this may sound like a weird

concept - emotional pain manifesting as physical pain and symptoms - but it's a very common one in Eastern Medicine, as well as
energy medicine.

Several years ago I had a patient who came to me with severe low
back pain. He was an older man but very active in his hiking and
cross country ski clubs. I knew he had some arthritis but he didn't
seem to be responding to treatment the way I thought he should.
It was in December and Christmas was approaching. During one
of his appointments he told me that he and his wife, children and
grandchildren were going to be getting together for their annual
holiday at their cabin. He also told me that it was going to be the
one year anniversary of his daughter's sudden death due to a car
crash. Interestingly, once he got through the anniversary date of
his daughter's passing, the low back pain abated. (Some details
were altered to protect my patient's identity.)

Anniversary dates are definitely something to be aware of. Birthdays, wedding anniversaries, etc. can bring back powerful memories and emotions. Mayo Clinic staff write, "When a loved one
dies, you might be faced with grief over your loss again and again
— sometimes even years later. Feelings of grief might return on
the anniversary of your loved one's death, birthday or other special days throughout the year. These feelings, sometimes called
an anniversary reaction, aren't necessarily a setback in the grieving process. They're a reflection that your loved one's life was important to you."[1] The day my Mom passed happened to be New
Year's Day. Needless to say there were a lot of days that year
(Valentine's Day, Easter, Mother's Day, her birthday, my parents'
wedding anniversary, even my own birthday, etc.) that triggered
grief which needed to be processed!

Other signs and symptoms of grief may include irritability, feeling emotionally numb, overreacting to day to day situations, over
eating, loss of appetite, excess alcohol intake, difficulty concen-

161

trating and experiencing anxiety and overwhelm. Physical symptoms of mourning can affect any body part or system. Again, from a Chinese medicine perspective, the lungs, large intestine and skin are seen as being responsible for helping process grief. Thus, as part of that processing, or lack thereof, bronchial or sinus infections or allergies can often get worse.

If we take the opportunity and have the proper support, the symptoms of grief should gradually lessen as the months pass with just a few activations such as on anniversary dates as I noted above. Sometimes, however, people get "stuck" in their grief and experience what is known as complicated grief.[2] This means that even months or years after a loved one's passing, for example, the grief feels as painful as if the event just happened. In extreme cases, people may feel suicidal, in which case, medical intervention is definitely needed.

Processing It: In Western culture within our family, community or in the corporate world, we do not deal well with grief. I remember years ago when my Grandmother passed away, the company who owned the clinic where I worked had a policy (like most corporations) that allowed you three days compassion leave. Seriously? I can tell you three days off to make travel arrangements, attend a funeral and help take care of sorting through personal and legal affairs of your loved one who has passed is definitely not enough. My Grandmother lived a two and a half hour flight away and I ended up using my holiday time to go home and attend her funeral and spend time with family. Clearly, whoever made that policy did not have an understanding of grief and the grieving process.

One of the things I like about Chinese medicine (the BodyTalk System incorporates many of these concepts) is that they acknowledge that we are all hardwired to experience joy and sadness (two sides to the same coin), worry, grief, fear and anger. They recognize that there is nothing wrong with feeling any of these emotions. What is important, however, is *how* the emotions get processed. For example, if a person experiencing grief is able to work through it in a healthy and supported manner, the result will be dispersion of the emotion. What this means is that if a person has lost a loved one, for example, they will be able to think about that person but not feel the intensity of the grief that they felt in the time immediately after their loved one had passed. Similarly, if a person has gone through a difficult divorce, over time there is a lessening of the emotional pain. This process can only happen if you allow yourself to feel the grief. Most of us want to avoid emotional pain so we rationalize it or worse, stuff it in a closet and try to pretend that it's not there and just bury ourselves in work or other distractions. Again, in Chinese medicine, if the grief is not processed in a healthy manner, this can lead to disintegration or in Western medicine what would be referred to as complicated grief.

It is also important to recognize that there are many layers to the grieving process. A number of years ago the elderly husband of a friend of mine passed away. My friend had been caring for him for many years as he had a chronic degenerative health condition. She was also very spiritual and was very intentional in processing her anticipatory grief through various avenues. On the day of her husband's funeral she was very calm and didn't shed a tear. Everyone commented on how well she was doing. I, on the other hand, was waiting for the other shoe to drop. Sure enough, three months after her husband passed she ended up taking a weekend workshop on the importance of breathing for physical, emotional and spiritual health. During one of the breathing exercises she said she started to weep uncontrollably and sobbed for several minutes. Afterwards, she was exhausted but also felt a great sense of release and letting go. Even though she had been very intentional about her anticipatory grieving process, there was still another layer to be dealt with after her husband's actual passing.

Dr. Jennifer Harrison

My father had Parkinson's disease and dementia. I knew that when he physically passed, which he did in 2013, I would feel like I had lost him twice; once with the dementia and then with his actual physical passing. I know others who have had parents go through Alzheimer's and they've said that they experienced the same thing - layers of grief.

Dr. Elizabeth Kübler-Ross was an American psychiatrist who did ground-breaking work on near-death experiences. In 1969, she wrote a book called *On Death and Dying*, of which a commemorative edition was published in 2014 on the 10th anniversary of her passing. In this top-selling book, she outlined the "Five Stages of Grief", namely denial, anger, bargaining, depression and acceptance. Over the years, these stages came to be accepted as "gospel" but have also come under attack for being too formulaic. In truth, Dr. Kübler-Ross noted that the stages were not meant to be a complete list of all possible emotions that could be felt, and that they could occur in any order. Regardless, I find it interesting to note that depression is a part of healthy grieving. In the past year I have had two healthy patients with no history of clinical depression be prescribed anti-depressants by their family doctors to "help" them cope with their grief. In one case, the patient was also referred for counseling but it was going to take several months before they could get in to see the psychologist. A couple of months after the patient started taking the anti-depressants they said to me how much better they were feeling and that they didn't think they needed to go for counseling. I had to tell the patient that although the medications were alleviating the depression that was actually part of the grieving process, the cause of the depression i.e. grief, needed to be addressed and I encouraged them to follow up with the counseling. While there is a time and a place for medications, I get concerned when a natural process such as depression as a part of grieving (which is not the same as clinical depression where a patient may be suicidal) gets disrupted by a prescription medication. Grieving is not a disease! It is a process and it is a natural part of life. However, in our Western culture, we typically do not deal well with the process. I've noticed over the past 10 years or so more and more people do not want funerals for themselves or for loved ones. This important ritual is being minimized for a variety of reasons.

Regardless of whether you've lost a loved one, gone through a painful divorce or are dealing with anticipatory grief (i.e. anticipating a loss), I really encourage you to take the time to process your grief. This may involve taking a grief and bereavement course at your church, religious centre, at a hospital or a counseling centre, talking to a counselor or just reading some books on grieving and journaling your feelings. Taking good care of yourself by getting adequate rest, good nutrition, gentle exercise and delegating responsibilities where you're able are all helpful steps to take.

Seeking out health care modalities like massage therapy, chiropractic, acupuncture, Reiki and BodyTalk may also be beneficial to you on your grieving journey. If you or someone you know appears to be "stuck" in their grief or have experienced several losses in a relatively short period of time, then seeing a medical doctor or psychologist may be needed. A woman I once knew had experienced three deaths in her family, one of her husband's relatives had died in a car crash, the company she worked for got bought out by another, management changed and she and her family moved to a new neighbourhood. All of this happened in the span of a year! It took her another year, but finally she was able to attend grief counseling to begin her healing journey.

Helping Others By Acknowledging Their Grief: None of us are alone! While processing grief may make us feel separated from others, every single person on the planet experiences grief in one form or another during their lifetime. It's a natural part of life. Just the way everyone processes grief differently, everyone receives consoling differently. Some are the "stiff upper lip" kind

Dr. Jennifer Harrison

who don't want any sympathy while others turn into a puddle of tears with a simple smile and kind word of condolence. Recognizing that a person may be grieving because they lost their job is just as important as acknowledging that someone has lost a loved one. Losing a pet can be as painful as other losses, human or otherwise. Offering sympathy may take us out of our comfort zone, but it may go a long way in helping someone else. Empathy, compassion and kindness are critical as we journey together through this thing called life.

RESOURCES:

1. http://www.mayoclinic.org/healthy-living/end-of-life/in-depth/grief/art-20045340
2. http://www.mayoclinic.org/diseases-conditions/complicated-grief/basics/definition/con-20032765

SECTION 5: MONEY AND ABUNDANCE

Dr. Jennifer Harrison

CHAPTER 42: SO, YOU WANT TO WIN THE LOTTERY?

Ok, so we've all fantasized about what we'd do if we won the lottery - pay off the mortgage, quit our day job, buy a new house and car, travel, give part of it away to charity, and the list goes on. What many people don't realize, however, is that, according to T. Harv Eker in his book *Secrets of the Millionaire Mind*, "regardless of the size of their winnings, most lottery winners eventually return to their original financial state."[1] Research shows that about 70 percent of lottery winners will eventually go broke. A study done of lottery winners in Florida found that out of 35,000 winners, more than 1,900 actually went bankrupt within five years – which is double the average of bankruptcies amongst non-lottery winners![2] This included people who won anywhere from $50,000 to $150,000. "Oh, this would never happen to me", you say. Well, that all depends on what Eker calls your "money blueprint" or how you've been programmed to handle money. Do you know what your money blueprint is? Do you know how to start attracting more money into your life? In this chapter I'll help you identify your money blueprint and also help you determine what your Christmas shopping budget should be. If it's less than you'd like it to be, no worries! You can take advantage of the hot tips I have for you in "Chapter 43: How to Have a Stress Free Christmas...Well, Almost".

In order to know what your money blueprint is, here's what you need to do. Check to see how much money you have in your bank accounts and then check to see how much money you owe in loans and credit card debt. Subtract the amount of money you owe from the amount of money you have, and that should give you an idea of what your money blueprint is. If you're in the red, that is, you owe more money than you have, that means your money blueprint is set for debt. If you're in the black, then your money blueprint is set for wealth.

169

Another indicator of what your money "thermostat" is set at is how much money you are currently earning and whether you pay all your bills, including your credit cards, every month. Are you living within your means? Do you even keep track of your monthly finances?

Well, common sense and research, not to mention the Universal Laws of Attraction, will tell you that if you can't manage the money you have now, you'll never be able to manage more money if it comes into your life. As we've already seen, this has been proven over and over again by lottery winners, not to mention professional athletes (78 percent of NFL players file for bankruptcy within five years of retirement).[3] So, where do you start?

Well, the best place to start is to keep track of your income, the money you receive every month from your job, business, or other sources. The next thing is to keep track of all your monthly expenses from rent/mortgage, utilities, groceries, to money you spend on clothing, movies and even coffee! "Oh, that sounds like too much work", you say. Well, I guess that lets you know what your money blueprint or thermostat is set at. Actually, it's pretty easy to keep track of your monthly expenses. Just open up an Excel spread sheet (or Numbers, if you're a Mac user). Make a list of all the expenses you have. Include everything! Here are some of the categories that I would recommend:

Rent/mortgage

Property taxes

Maintenance fees, if you live in a condo

Groceries and Household (you may want to make a separate line for things like alcohol, cigarettes and junk food if these are included in your monthly purchases)

Utilities itemized as phone, internet, cable, electricity, water, gas or by company

Loan payments: student loans, car payments, lines of credit, etc.

Insurance: house/condo/apartment, car, health, etc.

Gas, car maintenance and repairs

Transit costs

Service charges on your bank accounts (these can really add up)

Clothing

Entertainment: movies, dining out, coffee, going to the bar, video games, etc.

Personal: money spent on gifts for others, books, apps for your smart phone, etc.

Travel

Money you're putting into savings and investments

Donations to charity

You can customize the list as you need to. In order to really get a handle on your finances, you're going to have to keep track of your receipts for all your in-store and online purchases. Also, keep your credit card and bank statements. It shouldn't take you more than 60 minutes (the length of an episode of *Dancing with the Stars* or *Grey's Anatomy*) to:

1. Set up the Excel/Numbers spread sheet.

2. Print off your bank and credit card statements from online banking.

3. Input the numbers from your receipts, bank and credit card statements.

4. Add up the expenses.

5. Add up your monthly pay cheques/revenue.

Now, take a few minutes to look at not only the grand total of your expenses, but also where the money is going each month. Next, compare the grand total with your monthly paycheque/revenue. How do your numbers look? Where is your financial thermostat set? What is your money blueprint looking like?

Remember at the beginning I said I'd help you figure out what your Christmas shopping budget should be? Well, here is what you need to do. How much money did you have left over at the end of the month? This was the difference between what your monthly revenue was and what your expenses were. Have you been putting money away into a Christmas shopping fund? If you don't have any money left over – or worse, you're chronically going deeper and deeper into debt each month, then your Christmas shopping budget is zero! If you haven't been putting money away each month in anticipation of Holiday shopping and you're currently breaking even or actually losing money each month, then your Holiday shopping budget is also zero. This may come as a bit of a shock and you may not want to accept it. However, the numbers don't lie. If you don't have any money left over or set aside, the only way you'll pay for the extra Christmas expenses is by going (further) into debt.

Here's something important to note: if you're struggling with debt, particularly credit card debt, go speak to someone at your bank or a non-profit credit card counseling agency. Also, if your Christmas shopping budget is zero, don't despair! Check out some of the suggestions in the next chapter, "How to Have a Stress Free Christmas...Well, Almost".

Now that you have a budget that you can use each month, check to see where you can cut back on your expenses. A friend of mine shared with me recently that her husband gave up smoking once he realized that he was spending over \$400 a month just on cigarettes! If you're buying a specialty coffee every day, that could add up to more than \$120 a month, just on coffee! Saving \$120, let alone \$400, could go a long way in creating a healthy Christmas budget not to mention a positive money blueprint!

I hope these suggestions have been helpful for you. Financial stress is a huge burden. However, as you've seen if you looked at your monthly income and expenses, you can start to change your money blueprint. Getting a handle on properly managing the money you already have goes a long way in helping to decrease stress and increase wealth.

RESOURCES:

1. Eker, T. Harv. *Secrets of the Millionaire Mind*. New York: Harper Business, 2005.
2. http://www.marketwatch.com/story/why-lottery-winners-go-bankrupt-1301002181742
3. https://www.mint.com/blog/how-to/from-stoked-to-broke-why-are-so-many-professional-athletes-going-bankrupt-0213/?display=wide

Dr. Jennifer Harrison

CHAPTER 43: HOW TO HAVE A STRESS FREE CHRISTMAS...WELL, ALMOST

Research has shown that the Christmas Holiday Season can be one of the most stressful times of the year. Anyone who has been within a five kilometer radius of a shopping centre in the month of December knows what the Christmas rush is like. The crowds, the checkout lines, not to mention the crazy parking lots all add up to increased stress on top of an already hectic month. Even small town grocery stores can be filled with long line ups. Do you want to find out about 10 simple yet effective strategies to help you beat the Christmas rush? Would you like to decrease your stress and actually enjoy the holidays this year? Read on to find out how.

1. One of the most common stressors related to Christmas is over-spending. Money for gifts, groceries and travel can really take a toll. Know what your Christmas budget is. To borrow the phrase from the lottery commercials, "pick a limit and stay within it". In 2014, The National Retail Federation estimated that Americans would spend about $618 billion for the Holiday Season. In Canada, holiday shopping was expected to reach an estimated $90 billion. Spending this amount of money pushes many people even deeper into credit card debt, a place they can't afford to go. Financial stress can be crippling. If you are not sure what you can afford to spend on Christmas, you better take a look at your current monthly expenses. (See "Chapter 42: So, You Want to Win the Lottery?") How much do you spend on your mortgage/rent, food, utilities and loan payments? How much do you spend on clothing, entertainment, travel, even coffee? Whatever you have left over is what you've got for your Christmas budget. A more proactive strategy is to set aside some money in a savings account each month so your Christmas shopping budget is already available.

Dr. Jennifer Harrison

2. Once you've figured out what your holiday spending budget is, get all of your shopping done in November or earlier. You can take advantage of the pre-Christmas sales, plus decrease your stress in December!

3. Save money by purchasing decorations, gift wrap, gift bags, cards and stocking stuffers at your local dollar or discount store.

4. I know more and more families, especially ones with small children, who are choosing to limit gifts to two per person (including Mom and Dad); one "need" gift, like clothing, and one "wish list" gift like a toy, book or other fun item. By doing this, they are reinforcing the value of gratitude and the importance of spending time together. In other words, quality over quantity.

5. If you come from a large family or have a large group of friends you usually buy gifts for, instead of buying gifts for everyone, try drawing names instead. We did this in my family for years. All the adults (my parents, siblings and in-laws) would draw names and the children would all draw names amongst themselves. We also set a limit ($25) for each gift. This made it both fun and manageable. (Of course my Mom and Dad still bought gifts for all the grandchildren!)

6. Do a fun gift exchange game "recycling" items from your home that you're not using like kitchen items, books, vases, scarves, jewellery, etc. According to organizing expert Jillian Pollock, 80 percent of what we keep, we never use! We did this one year in my family and we had a blast! (I ended up with a salad spinner from my Mom which was something I actually needed, wanted, still have and use!) We also do this for my workplace Christmas party.

7. In your family or group of friends, pick a theme, get creative and make your gifts. Lots of inexpensive, simple and fun ideas can be found on web sites like HGTV and Pinterest.

8. Instead of exchanging gifts with your group of friends, have a charity bake sale instead. A friend of mine and her neighbours do this every year. They've literally generated thousands of dollars over the years for worthwhile charities. Plus, everyone has fun and gets baking for the holidays!

9. Forfeit gifts altogether and donate money and time to your favourite charity over the holidays. You can make it a group effort by doing this with your family and/or friends.

10. Take advantage of post-Christmas sales. You can purchase items needed for next Christmas, often for 75 percent or more off the original price. Also, clothing and household items are significantly discounted. I know some people who actually wait until after Christmas to buy gifts for their family. On Christmas Day each family member gets their fun stocking stuffers. However, they also get a picture or "coupon" for the actual gift they'll be receiving. It extends the fun and saves a ton of money. Plus, it reduces the stress of shopping for everything in the few short weeks before Christmas.

I hope this chapter has given you some solid and fun options to beat the Christmas rush. By using some of these strategies it can help you decrease stress (including financial stress) but more importantly, allow you to remember the real reason for the season. Regardless of your spiritual or religious affiliation, I think we can all agree that spending quality time with family and friends and extending Good Will to All is a great way to have a stress free Christmas!

Dr. Jennifer Harrison

CHAPTER 44: CREDIT CARDS - FRIEND OR FOE?

When you get your credit card statements in January (or any month, for that matter) and you look at the total amount you owe, will you feel like it's no big deal or will you be on the verge of total panic with no clue as to how you're going to pay off this debt? If you didn't curb your Christmas spending and you blew through your budget (assuming you had one), you may be feeling that your credit cards are definitely the enemy at the moment. Debt is one of the leading causes of stress. According to TransUnion, the average Canadian consumer debt (which excludes mortgages but includes, credit cards, car loans and lines of credit) has risen to $27,355 per person of which $3,573 is credit card debt. In the US, credit card debt is an average of $7,128 per person. In Canada as of December, 2013, the total consumer credit debt was $505 billion. In the United States as of October, 2013, that number is $3.076 trillion. Staggering! However, the good news is that there are ways to turn it around if you're willing to replace some bad spending habits with some good ones! This chapter will give you some strategies to help change your credit cards from foes to friends!

First of all, it *is* possible to have your credit cards be your "friends". However, it requires that you already have disciplined money spending habits, have a budget that you constantly keep track of and that you live within your means. If you have these things in place, then you can take advantage of earning reward points with your credit card to put toward trips, merchandise or even cash back, for example. If you don't fall into this category, read on.

According to a CTV interview given by Jeffrey Schwartz, executive director of Consolidated Credit Counselling Services of Canada, there are some simple steps you can take to get yourself out of debt.

Dr. Jennifer Harrison

1. First of all, if you're drowning in debt, get help! There are a number of non-profit debt counselling services. In my research, I found a Government of Canada (Financial Consumer Agency of Canada) web page that can help you with this. http://www.fcac-acfc.gc.ca/eng/resources/publications/budgeting/Pages/GettingH-Obtenirl.aspx#agency

2. Stop using your credit cards! How can you get out of debt if you keep accumulating it? The average Canadian is spending $1.65 for every $1 of disposable income. The way I look at it, it's like having a pile of garbage bags on your kitchen floor and each week you take out one bag but then add almost two more. You would never do this in your home, so why do it with your money?

3. Make your debt repayment plan "invisible". What that means is have automatic payments come off your pay cheque or out of your account each month so that you don't have to think about it. A credit counselling service can help you with this. You can do the same thing for savings. For example, you can arrange with your bank to have a set amount come out of your chequing account each month that goes directly to your RRSPs, TFSA (in Canada) or savings account. The amount remaining in your account is what you have left for your other monthly expenses.

4. Plan ahead. Create a monthly budget by calculating what your income is and what your monthly expenses are for the necessities like rent/mortgage, food, utilities and loan payments. (See "Chapter 42: So, You Want to Win the Lottery?") Factor in extra expenses that can come up for things like house and car repairs or holidays.

5. Set a goal. A credit counsellor can help you create a tangible, attainable goal for debt repayment. Mr. Schwartz recommends three and a half to four years. (See "Chapter 5: New Year's Resolutions vs Goal Setting" for some additional tips.)

Getting your credit card debt under control is a great way to Go From Your Stressed Self to Your Best Self™!

RESOURCES:

1. http://www.fcac-acfc.gc.ca/eng/resources/publications/budgeting/Pages/GettingH-Obtenirl.aspx#agency
2. http://www.ctvnews.ca/business/household-debt-in-canada-hits-all-time-high-but-may-be-nearing-limit-1.1590905
3. http://www.theglobeandmail.com/globe-investor/personal-finance/household-finances/average-canadian-consumer-debt-climbs-to-25597-but-toronto-and-vancouver-buck-the-trend/article15411223/
4. http://www.huffingtonpost.ca/2013/01/14/credit-card-debt-canada-interest-rate_n_2468816.html
5. http://www.nerdwallet.com/blog/credit-card-data/average-credit-card-debt-household/
6. https://www.youtube.com/watch?v=3r66qETVd5A (Jeffrey Schwartz interview on CTV)

Dr. Jennifer Harrison

CHAPTER 45: MONEY MATTERS

Have you received your credit card bills this month? Are you dreading what the amount owed will be? Do you even know what the amount will be? One of the key stressors that affect people is worrying about money. However, as much as people worry about their finances, it doesn't always translate into making necessary changes to improve their financial status. Well, just like anything else, it's all about habits. With money, that involves your spending as well as your saving habits. Did you know that there are actually different money "personalities"? Money does matter and it plays a significant role in contributing to our stress levels as well as our enjoyment of life. In this chapter I'm going to help you identify which money personality you may be and how you can use that information to help with your money matters.

One way to look at our financial habits is to think about money personalities: spenders, savers, spiritual types and avoiders. Let's take a look at each one and see which one most resonates with you.

Spenders: Whenever spenders have extra money, it's gone, usually spent on things like clothes, eating out at expensive restaurants and on vehicles that are more extravagant than they actually need. Sometimes, they spend money on gifts for other people. Now I'm not saying that there is anything wrong with spending money on nice clothes, cars or buying gifts for family and friends. The problem comes when the spending *exceeds* their income and is not balanced with saving and donating to charity. Also, they typically don't keep track of their spending and frequently run into issues like maxing out their credit cards. They often have difficulty paying back their loans.

Savers: These people are the opposite of spenders. They are always saving their money "for a rainy day". When they do make purchases, it always has to be the cheapest price, even if that means poor quality. Savers are like the hoarders you see on the TV reality shows. They tend to be afraid that they'll lose all their money and often don't allow themselves to enjoy things that money can buy. They also tend to be less than generous when it comes to donating money to charity or helping a friend or family member.

Spiritual Types: These are the people who believe the misinterpretation of the Bible verse "money is the root of all evil". The actual verse from 1 Timothy 6:10 is "For the love of money is the root of all kinds of evil, and in their eagerness to be rich some have wandered away from the faith and pierced themselves with many pains." They believe that having a lot of money automatically means being greedy, therefore it is impossible to be a spiritual person *and* be rich. So, whenever they do have money, they either spend it or give it away. They tend to always be scraping by, but deep down believe that they are better people than those who are wealthy.

Avoiders: They tend to steer clear of managing their money. They don't keep track of their spending or saving. Avoiders, particularly when in a relationship, often let their partner look after anything that has to do with money such as paying the bills and making the investments. Out of sight, out of mind. Sometimes they can tend to take on a bit of a spiritual type of approach and rely on God or The Universe to provide the money they need to pay the rent or pay for the vacation they just booked using money they don't have.

After taking a look at these different money personalities, which one are you? What are the disadvantages and advantages of these approaches to managing money?

As you can see, there are fundamental flaws with each of the money personalities. The spenders create stress for themselves and their families by continually being in debt. Savers tend to create stress for themselves by worrying that something terrible is going to happen so they better save up "just in case." Even when they do spend their money on necessary things like food or even fun things like a vacation, they are not able to enjoy it. Spiritual types, ironically, miss the point that the more money you have, the more opportunities you have to be generous and help other people. They see people like Warren Buffet and Oprah Winfrey as being evil greedy people and fail to see how generous they've been with their wealth and how much they have helped others. Avoid-ers typically live in fear. If they're not in control of their money then they can't make mistakes with it. The problem is that in-stead of being informed and proactive, they often create more fi-nancial problems and stress by not actively managing their money.

There are also some advantages to each of the personality types. The spenders help the economy move forward. If people don't spend money, that hurts the economy. For example, if you work for a company that makes vacuum cleaners but no one buys them, then the company goes out of business and you lose your job. The savers help to avoid the stress that comes with creating and car-rying too much debt. The spiritual types tend to make ethical de-cisions in the way they earn and spend their money. The avoiders often end up attracting money in miraculous ways because of their belief and faith that money will appear when needed.

Earlier, I asked which money personality you think applies to you? Well, the reality is that most of us are a predominant type but we also have traits of the others personalities. The way we deal with money is highly influenced by our parents. We either end up managing money the way they did, or we do the exact op-posite. For example, if your parents were miserly with their money, you may tend to be a saver or hoarder. However, some-times people react by being the opposite and spending whatever money they have, whenever they have it, even if that means in-curring a lot of debt. Deep down they believe that because they were deprived growing up that the world now owes them. It's also important to realize that most people have no conscious aware-ness of their belief systems around money. However, the more awareness you have, the better you can manage your money and decrease the stress that comes from poor money habits.

Ideally, balance is the key – pun intended. It is important to be able to save money, not only for your retirement, but also for other things like education, vacations and necessities, as well as chari-table donations to help others. It's important to spend wisely and live within your means. It's important to earn and spend your money ethically and with integrity. It also helps to have faith when setting financial goals and implementing healthy money management strategies. Being grateful for all the money you have now goes a long way in helping to put things in perspective and to decrease stress.

Well, I hope that looking at how you deal with money from a money personality perspective has been useful. The more aware-ness you have about your money habits, the better financial deci-sions you can make. It's also a great way to Go From Your Stressed Self To Your Best Self™!

RESOURCES:

1. Eker, T Harv. *Secrets of the Millionaire Mind*. New York: Harper Business, 2005.
2. Hansen, Mark Victor and Allen, Robert G. *The One Minute Millionaire*. New York: Harmony Books, 2002.
3. https://www.srpl.net/there-are-4-money-personalities-whats-yours/

SECTION 6: THE BIGGER PICTURE

Dr. Jennifer Harrison

CHAPTER 46: CAN MEDITATION CREATE WORLD PEACE?

It's been speculated that meditation has been around since the dawn of civilization. Meditation has been and continues to be a spiritual practice across many faiths from Christianity, Judaism and Islam to Buddhism, Hinduism, Taoism as well as New Age and Pagan practices. More recently we've been hearing about the health benefits of meditation. According to the Mayo Clinic and Harvard University, some research suggests that meditation may help people manage symptoms of conditions such as: anxiety disorders, asthma, cancer, depression, heart disease, high blood pressure, pain and sleep problems.[1,2] However, can meditation create world peace?

When asked how to create world peace, Mother Teresa is quoted as saying, "Go home and love your family." There is much truth to this. However, it is also easier said than done. Interestingly, a number of studies have been done using group transcendental meditation (TM) to see if crime rates, conflict and economic trends could be changed.[3] While there are many types of meditation (See "Chapter 1: Meditation - Which Type is Right for You?"), TM focuses on clearing the mind and experiencing inner peace. One well known study led by Dr. John Hagelin, who is a professor of physics and director of the Institute of Science, Technology and Public Policy at Maharishi University of Management, took place in Washington, DC, in the summer of 1993. From June 7 to July 30, a group of trained meditators, which started at around 800 and rose to 4000, meditated. At the time, Washington, DC's crime rate was three times the national average. Over the course of the meditation study, the crime rate decreased by 23.3 percent.[4]

Another interesting study was done near Liverpool, England. A crime prevention study showed that a group of specialist meditators reduced crime in Liverpool by a comparative 58 percent when the numbers in the group equalled the square root of one percent of the local population.[5] Yes, there is even a mathematical formula that calculates the "magic number" of meditators needed to create a measurable difference!

So what does that mean for us? What can we do on a daily basis to help create world peace? Well, I think like with most things, it has to start from within. What I mean by that is that we have to start creating our own inner peace if we hope to have a measurable impact on our outer world. We are all connected in ways beyond what most of us can comprehend. As a simple example, have you ever been having a rotten day and you go to a store and the sales person is extra friendly? Maybe they even go out of their way to be helpful or just make a comment that makes you laugh? You leave the store feeling much better than when you entered. What changed? You experienced the effect of another person's positive outlook and behaviour. In turn, it changed your outlook and behaviour, maybe even to the extent that when you went home you were nice to your family instead of taking out your rotten day on them. It may seem like a little thing, but it's very powerful.

When you meditate and feel more peaceful, this energy has a radiating effect, not only on you, but the people around you. Now imagine hundreds or even thousands of people all meditating together. It's like the ripple effect of a stone being dropped into a pool of water. So, again, what does this mean for you? How can you start to make changes in your own life through meditation? Well, there are many meditation CDs, DVDs and YouTube videos out there, not to mention Apple and Android apps – some of which are free. Plus, there are different meditation classes that can teach you how to meditate. As I mentioned previously, there are also many ways to meditate besides TM. So whether you are wanting to create world peace, peace in your community or even peace in your own family, why not start with creating your own inner peace? You will be amazed at the results!

RESOURCES:

off

off

off

off

peace in your own family, why not start with creating your own inner peace? You will be amazed at the results!

RESOURCES:

1. http://www.mayoclinic.org/tests-procedures/meditation/in-depth/meditation/art-20045858
2. http://www.health.harvard.edu/blog/mindfulness-meditation-may-ease-anxiety-mental-stress-201401086967
3. http://www.davidlynchfoundation.org/bibliography.html
4. http://www.worldpeacegroup.org/washington_crime_prevention_full_article.html
5. http://www.worldpeacegroup.org/liverpool_crime_study.html

Dr. Jennifer Harrison

CHAPTER 47: CAN YOU BE ANGRY AND SPIRITUAL AT THE SAME TIME?

How often does something really tick you off? Has a family member or co-worker caused you to feel frustrated, maybe to the point where you lost your cool? Did you perhaps say things in anger that you regretted afterwards? Have you ever been angry but talked yourself out of expressing the anger because you felt it would be wrong, that it wouldn't be very polite or "spiritual" to do so? In this chapter I want to address some misconceptions about anger and how anger can actually be a positive thing in your life.

Over the years I've noticed, particularly in my practice and when I'm doing BodyTalk, that people are holding on to a lot of anger and frustration. In further conversation, I hear people say, "Oh, I was so angry but I decided to focus on gratitude and love instead." Or, "I'm just going to let it go to the Universe and not let the situation bother me anymore." While there is a lot to be said about focusing on love and gratitude and letting things go, these strategies can be extremely unhealthy in the long run and lead to even more anger building up if the anger itself is not first processed in a healthy way. "But, it's not spiritual to be angry. Anger is a negative emotion and therefore a bad thing," you say. Well, I'd like to share a different perspective with you.

There are a lot of Chinese medicine concepts incorporated into the BodyTalk System. BodyTalk is an energy medicine, consciousness based WholeHealthcare™ system that was developed over 20 years ago. I have been studying BodyTalk since 2001 and became a Certified BodyTalk Practitioner in 2002. Within Chinese medicine they see the emotions of joy, sadness, worry, grief, fear and anger as being associated with the Five Elements of Fire, Earth, Metal, Water and Wood. The Five Elements are a way of looking at how energy or qi flows through and affects our bodies and minds. In turn, it is believed that certain organs and body parts are responsible for processing the different emotions. The key thing to realize here is that, as human beings, we are all hard-wired to experience each of these emotions, pleasant or not. In addition, it's how the emotions get processed that is the most important thing. For example, with regard to anger, most people fall into two general categories:

1. Those who do not express their anger, keep it inside, avoid it by focusing of "positive" emotions instead and who come across as being very "spiritual". This is implosive behaviour.

2. Those who are angry all the time, prone to angry outbursts, sometimes to the point of being abusive. This is explosive behavior.

Now, granted, these are two extremes. However, I think we can appreciate both categories, either because we can relate to one of them, know people who fit the categories perfectly or because we bounce back and forth between the two. What I'd like to share with you is how you can process anger in a healthier manner by actually combining aspects of these two categories.

First of all, if you feel angry about something, acknowledge that you are angry! That doesn't mean that you shout obscenities or break every dish in the kitchen. However, what it means is that you acknowledge the emotion of anger. It means that you express that anger in an appropriate way which may involve some shouting, strong words, or throwing a pillow around. This may happen when another person is present or when you are by yourself. Sometimes it is a situation, not a specific person that makes you feel angry.

Second of all, write down how you're feeling without editing anything. Let it all out! I prefer writing to typing on the computer because different areas of the brain are activated when we are writing compared to typing. However, do which ever works best for you.

Once you have it all out on paper, reflect on what the trigger was that caused you to feel angry in the first place. Was the trigger really the trigger or did you "shoot the messenger" and misdirect your anger toward something or someone who wasn't directly involved in the situation? When have you felt angry about a similar situation in the past? Is there a pattern? Were you really feeling fearful but the reaction was anger instead? What role did you play in the situation? Yes, as much as we want to blame someone or something else, if we really want to work through the anger, we have to acknowledge our role in it, too.

Again, from a Chinese medicine perspective, they see the healthy processing of anger leading to movement. Expressing anger in a proper manner helps to "clear the air, dispel tension and restore(s) balance."[1] If anger is not processed properly, it leads to explosiveness which can be harmful to our bodymind health.

From a spiritual perspective, I often remind people that even Jesus got angry and really angry. In the Gospel of Matthew 21:12, it says that "Jesus entered the Temple and began to drive out all the people buying and selling animals for sacrifice. He knocked over the tables of the money changers and the chairs of those selling doves." No, he did not hold back! To put things in an historical context, Jesus got angry because the selling of animals for sacrifice had turned into a real money making racket and people were missing the point about honouring God.

The key take home point is that, as human beings, spiritual or otherwise, we're all going to experience anger. However, the most important thing is how it gets processed. Dealing with anger in a healthy manner goes a long way in helping you Go From Your Stressed Self to Your Best Self™!

195

Dr. Jennifer Harrison

RESOURCES:

1. Elias, Jason and Ketcham, Katherine. *Chinese Medicine for Maximum Immunity: Understanding the Five Elemental Types for Health and Well-being.* New York: Three Rivers Press, 1998.

CHAPTER 48: CANCER - A FRESH PERSPECTIVE

April is Cancer Awareness Month. I think everyone has been af-fected by cancer either directly or by having a friend, co-worker or family member diagnosed with the disease. I know some people currently living with cancer. I've had patients, friends and ex-tended family members die from cancer. I've had four friends who have had cancer, recovered and never looked back. Everyone's journey is unique.

This month I want to highlight the amazing journey of Anita Moorjani, author of the international bestseller *Dying To Be Me: My Journey From Cancer, To Near Death, To True Healing*, who shows us what is possible if we live from a place of love and let go of fear.

On April 26, 2002, she was diagnosed with lymphoma. It is a deadly form of cancer and over the next four years she searched out and received many forms of treatment from modern medical care to ancient healing techniques and everything in between. However, on February 2, 2006, she was rushed, yet again to the hospital, only this time the doctors said there was nothing else they could do and that her death was imminent. However, instead of dying, she went into a coma and had a near death experience or NDE. She documents this wonderful, life changing experience in her book. The powerful lesson she learned during that time was that the most important thing is LOVE. "Love, joy, ecstasy, and awe poured into me, through me, and engulfed me. I was swal-lowed up and enveloped in more love than I ever knew existed. I felt more free and alive than I even had. ... The feeling of com-plete, pure, unconditional love was unlike anything I'd known be-fore...it was totally undiscriminating, as if I didn't have to do an-ything to deserve it, nor did I need to prove myself to earn it."[1] Essentially what happened after she regained consciousness was that, within five weeks, she was released from the hospital and there was no evidence of cancer anywhere in her body! Medical

197

doctors and researchers from around the world have studied her case. Thankfully, best-selling author Dr. Wayne Dyer and others encouraged her to share her life affirming story of how she moved from living in fear, which she feels is what caused her cancer, to living in love in her book *Dying To Be Me*, a must-read for everyone, in my opinion.

On her web site, she has posted her TEDx Bay Area talk. I hope you enjoy her words of wisdom, which can be summed up by saying Live from a Place of Love, not a Place of Fear.

RESOURCES:

1. Moorjani, Anita. *Dying To Be Me: My Journey From Cancer, To Near Death, To True Healing*. Carlsbad, California: Hay House Publishing, 2012. pp. 65-66.
2. http://www.anitamoorjani.com/about-anita/

CHAPTER 49: ANGELS - MYTH OR REALITY?

According to a 2011 poll, of the 1000 Americans interviewed, 77 percent believed that angels were real.[1] A similar 2007 poll of 1000 Canadians showed that 66 percent believed in angels.[2] As the Christmas Season approaches, angels inevitably pop up everywhere from Bible scripture readings in church, to Christmas tree decorations, to the carols we sing, to the movies we watch like the classic *It's a Wonderful Life.* While stories of angels actually span many of the world's various religions and cultures, how is it that over the millennia, angels continue to have such a popular place in our lives? Are they real or simply a myth to help us feel better in a troubled world? Have you ever had an encounter with an ethereal angel? In this chapter I'm going to explore both the spiritual and the scientific side to the question, Angels: Myth or Reality?

Back in 1967, Gustav Davidson, an award winning author, editor and consultant to the Kennedy Foundation on angelology (the study of angels) published his book called *A Dictionary of Angels, Including the Fallen Angels.*[3] He never intended to compile all this information. It just started out as an interest in collecting books on angels. In his book he cites hundreds of angels who have been named in literally hundreds of sources over the millennia. From A to Z, there are named angels who appear across the world's religions and cultures. He notes that St. Augustine is quoted as saying, "Every visible thing in this world is put under the charge of an angel." His dictionary certainly brings to light the significant role that angels have played through the ages.

In 1990, Sophy Burnham published *A Book of Angels.*[4] In the forward of her book she explains that the book started out as a bit of an autobiography for herself and her friends. She realized at age 43 that she'd had many mysterious things occur to her over the years that she just couldn't dismiss any longer. They could not be explained in a logical way. "How could I ignore the fact that my

199

own life had been saved in a miraculous fashion? Or that strange coincidences and meetings seemed to occur?...This book began, then, as...stories of things that had either happened to me personally or to friends so close that I could attest to their sanity. Each encounter is true. The book has grown, now, and changed, as I have, and includes encounters with angels from all over the world."

In 1992, Joan Webster Anderson published her book called *Where Angels Walk*.[5] On Christmas Eve, 1983, Joan's son and his friend were driving when their car broke down on the side of the road. No one was out because of the record breaking wind chill of -80F. They ended up having a mystical experience of being rescued on the side of a deserted road by a tow truck driver who, after dropping them off at their friend's house, mysteriously disappeared without a trace, including leaving no tire tracks in the snow. As time passed, Joan was prompted to do research on angels. While she found out historical as well as fictional information about angels, she wanted to know if angels actually existed now, in the present. So, she wrote to a number of magazines, who were already familiar with her newspaper and magazine articles, to ask if they would publish a letter she had written. Her letter said, "I am looking for people who believe they may have met an angel. I am talking about spirits who appeared in human form to give some kind of help. Please write to me at this box number..." (Obviously pre-internet.) To her amazement, she ended up receiving many letters from people, so many, in fact, that she ended up writing this book where she shares people's real life experiences with angels.

Dr. Doreen Virtue, "a spiritual doctor of psychology"[6] has written over 50 books on angels and has appeared on many TV shows including Oprah, CNN and The View. She has dedicated her life to helping people work with angels. On her web site she states, "Angel Therapy is a non-denominational spiritual healing method that involves working with a person's guardian angels and arch-angels, to heal and harmonize every aspect of life. Angel Therapy also helps you to more clearly receive Divine Guidance from the Creator and angels."

In January, 2014, Dr. Oz had Rebecca Rosen, a psychic medium and author, on his show to talk about how angels can help us to heal.[7] She ended up doing a reading with Dr. Oz, as well as two audience members which contained information that she had no way of knowing. Rebecca talked about how angels are messengers from God, beings of light to protect, comfort and heal us if we're open to letting them. Dr. Oz showed brain scans that illustrate the changes that physically happen in the brain when you medi-tate. She talked about using prayer, meditation and trust to con-nect with angels and to receive divine messages.

In September, 2014, a study was done to see whether the belief in guardian angels would cause people to take more risks. The study results were published in the journal *SAGE Open*. "While some felt that belief in guardian angels might make their behavior more risky, most believers were far less inclined to take risks than their non-believing counterparts."[8]

So, what does this all mean? Are angels just a myth or are they real? Well, yes! There is no question that much that has been writ-ten about angels over the centuries has been based on myth. How-ever, there are so many documented cases of people having real life experiences with angels, including valid mediums who can connect easily with them, that, in my mind, it's impossible to dis-pute that they exist. Even in quantum physics, nothing exists without an observer. What that means is that seeing is believing! So, whether or not you believe in angels is up to you. However, I think there is a reason that they continue to permeate many reli-gions as well as pop culture. I also believe that if we look in the mirror and are honest with ourselves, we can admit that we've all

Dr. Jennifer Harrison

had at least one experience in our lives that could only be explained by the presence of an angel.

RESOURCES:

1. http://www.cbsnews.com/news/poll-nearly-8-in-10-americans-believe-in-angels/
2. http://www.canada.com/story.html?id=9e9a3d24-e28e-4679-8797-81353e8c4291
3. Davidson, Gustav. *A Dictionary of Angels including the fallen angels.* New York: The Free Press, 1967.
4. Burnham, Sophy. *A Book of Angels.* New York: Ballantine Books, 1990.
5. Webster Anderson, Joan. *Where Angels Walk.* New York: Ballantine Books, 1992.
6. http://www.angeltherapy.com/about.php
7. http://www.doctoroz.com/episode/does-belief-angels-have-power-heal
8. http://www.ahchealthenews.com/2014/09/24/belief-in-guardian-angels-cuts-down-on-risky-behavior/

CHAPTER 50: IS THERE LIFE AFTER DEATH?

One of the biggest fears people have is the fear of dying. Will it involve a long, drawn out painful disease, will it be from an unexpected accident or will it be a peaceful passing when we're old and grey? What about after we die? Is that it? Is that all there is? Whether it be in the front of our minds (usually brought to the forefront when someone we know dies) or lurking in the background, this type of fear can cause a lot of stress and actually prevent us from enjoying our life in the present. So, is there life after death? While we often look to spiritual leaders for answers, you may be surprised by what science has to say!

In the Christian tradition, Easter is very much focused on life after death and indeed a resurrection. In looking at the season of spring, we see the earth come back to life after a long, cold winter (at least in Canada this year!). So, what about our own lives? What happens when we die? Is that the end? Do we really only live once? Well, in this chapter I would like to share with you the research and experience of three people: Dr. Gary Schwartz, Dr. Eben Alexander and Anita Moorjani.

Dr. Gary Schwartz is a professor of psychology, medicine, neurology, psychiatry and surgery at the University of Arizona and director of its Laboratory for Advances in Consciousness and Health. He is also corporate director of development of energy healing for Canyon Ranch Resorts and the author of several books, including: *The Sacred Promise, The Afterlife Experiments, The G.O.D. Experiments, The Truth about Medium, The Energy Healing Experiments*, and the coauthor of *The Living Energy Universe*. He has authored or coauthored more than 450 scientific papers including six in the journal *Science*, and has coedited 11 academic books. He is a Fellow of the American Psychological Society, the American Psychological Society, the Academy of Behavioral Medicine Research, and the Society of Behavioral Medicine.

Dr. Jennifer Harrison

He has appeared on hundreds of television and radio programs including HBO, Discovery, Arts & Entertainment, and NPR.[1]

In his book *The Afterlife Experiments: Breakthrough Scientific Evidence of Life After Death*, Dr. Schwartz risked his academic reputation and career by asking some well-known mediums (people who are able to communicate with those who have passed on) to become part of a series of experiments that ended up being done over a three year period to prove, or disprove, the existence of an afterlife and to see if there really is a continuation of consciousness after we physically die. What happened through these experiments was that evidence continued to pile up supporting the theory that, indeed, physical death is not the end. However, due to his rigorous scientific training, years as a researcher and even his own upbringing, he continued to be skeptical of the results, even though the majority of the data continued to support that our consciousness does continue on after physical death. Not only that, but that the consciousness of those who have passed on could be accessed by certain people such as the mediums who took part in the experiments. In his book, he says that he was avoiding looking at what the data as a whole was actually telling him. "The truth is that I was being scientifically hypocritical. I had failed to do the very thing I always try to encourage my students and colleagues to do."[2] Finally, after facing the fear of what it would mean for him as a man of science to actually "believe" what the data was telling him, that there really appeared to be life after death, he realized that he had to share what he and his co-researchers had experienced so he wrote the book *The Afterlife Experiments*.

Dr. Eben Alexander is a renowned academic and neurosurgeon who, over his career, has worked at several respected research hospitals including Harvard Medical School. He is a scientist who has spent most of his professional life firmly believing that although the near death experiences, or NDEs, that people claimed to have experienced felt real, they were simply fantasies created by the brain under extreme stress. However, one day, his own brain was attacked by a rare form of meningitis and the part of the brain that controls thought and emotion shut down completely. Most people who contract this type of infection rapidly decline and 90 percent die. The few who do survive the infection end up needing 24 hour a day care for the rest of their lives. What happened to Dr. Alexander is that after being in a coma for seven days, with his medical doctors ready to give up on any further treatment, he opened his eyes. Not only that, he made a full recovery! This, in and of itself, is a medical miracle. However, on top of all that, while he was in a coma, he had a powerful near death experience where he "journeyed beyond this world and encountered an angelic being who guided him into the deepest realms of super-physical existence. There he met, and spoke with, the Divine source of the universe itself...Before he underwent his journey, he could not reconcile his knowledge of neuroscience with any belief in heaven, God, or the soul. Today Dr. Alexander is a doctor who believes that true health can be achieved only when we realize that God and the soul are real and that death is not the end of personal existence but only a transition."[3, 4] Dr. Alexander's amazing experience is documented in his book, *Proof of Heaven: A Neurosurgeon's Journey into the Afterlife.*

Anita Moorjani is the author of the international bestseller *Dying To Be Me: My Journey From Cancer, To Near Death, To True Healing.* I shared her story in "Chapter 48: Cancer - A Fresh Perspective" but I would like to share it again here. On April 26, 2002, she was diagnosed with lymphoma. It is a deadly form of cancer and over the next four years she searched out and received many forms of treatment from modern medical care to ancient healing techniques and everything in between. However, her health continued to deteriorate and on February 2, 2006, she was rushed, yet again to the hospital, only this time the doctors said there was nothing else they could do and that her death was imminent. However, instead of dying, she went into a coma for 20

Dr. Jennifer Harrison

hours and had a near death experience (NDE). She documents this wonderful, life changing experience in her book. The powerful lesson she learned during that time was that the most important thing is LOVE. "Love, joy, ecstasy, and awe poured into me, through me, and engulfed me. I was swallowed up and enveloped in more love than I ever knew existed. I felt more free and alive than I ever had. ... The feeling of complete, pure, unconditional love was unlike anything I'd known before...it was totally undiscriminating, as if I didn't have to do anything to deserve it, nor did I need to prove myself to earn it."[5] Essentially what happened after she regained consciousness was that within five weeks she was released from the hospital and there was no evidence of cancer anywhere in her body! Medical doctors and researchers from around the world have studied her case. Thankfully, she was inspired to share her life and love affirming story of how she moved from living in fear, which she feels is what caused her cancer, to living in love in her book *Dying To Be Me*, a must-read for everyone, in my opinion.

I hope the stories of these three amazing people inspire you to not only read their books, but to look at both life and death differently. To release the fear of death is truly a life affirming experience!

RESOURCES:

1. http://www.drgaryschwartz.com/
2. Schwartz, Gary E., Simon, William L. *The Afterlife Experiments: Breakthrough Scientific Evidence of Life After Death.* New York: Atria Books, 2002. p. 256.
3. Alexander, Eben. *Proof of Heaven: A Neurosurgeon's Journey into the Afterlife.* New York: Simon and Schuster, 2012. (Back cover)
4. http://www.ebenalexander.com/

5. Moorjani, Anita. *Dying to Be Me: My Journey From Cancer, To Near Death, To True Healing.* Carlsbad, California: Hay House Publishing, 2012. pp. 65-66.
6. http://www.anitamoorjani.com/

Dr. Jennifer Harrison

CHAPTER 51: THE POWER OF INTENTION - MORE THAN MEETS THE EYE

We experience the world with our five senses: seeing, hearing, smelling, tasting and touching. In particular, our sense of sight and touch lead us to believe that we live in a concrete, material, mechanistic world. When we observe the events of our lives, they may appear to be very random. Sometimes it appears that we don't have any input or control at all regarding what happens to us. However, what if I were to tell you that our focus and intention actually do help to shape and create our lives? What if I told you that there is more here than meets the eye? In this chapter I want to share some mind blowing research as well as some practical action steps that can help us all be more conscious, intentional creators.

Dr. Wayne Dyer, in his book *The Power of Intention: Learning to Co-Create Your World Your Way*, talks about two different ways of looking at intention. One way is to perceive it as a single minded way of approaching life. He writes, "If you're one of those people with a never-give-up attitude combined with an internal picture that propels you toward fulfilling your dreams, you fit this description of someone with intention."[1] However, he goes on to talk about his own journey to a new, more spiritual understanding of intention. He shares that it's not just about an ego-driven pursuit of goals, but rather a spirit-guided approach to intentionally co-creating your life. "Intention is a power that's present everywhere as a field of energy." This may be a totally new way of perceiving things for you. Depending on your vantage point, it may sound like a bunch of New Age nonsense. However, for decades now, science has been exploring and discovering various fields of energy. For example, when you have an ECG (electrocardiogram), the electrical energy of the heart can be measured by putting electrodes on your chest. However, there are also devices that can measure the electromagnetic field of the heart up to 15 feet away from the body. Further research done by the Institute of HeartMath and others has shown that the heart's electromagnetic field actually stores information about what's happening in the body. This energy field is highly influenced by our thoughts and emotions, especially the ones we focus upon.[2] Other research investigates much broader energy fields.

Lynne McTaggart in her book, *The Intention Experiment: Using Your Thoughts to Change Your Life and Your World,* talks about research that was done at the Princeton Engineering Anomalies Research (PEAR) lab at Princeton University over 25 years that showed how people's thoughts and intentions could actually influence outputs of computers that were programmed to create randomly alternating images.[3] These computers are known as random event generators (REGs). The computers are programmed so that each image is shown repeatedly numerous times such that each image should show up 50 percent of the time. However, when people focused on one image over the other, they actually influenced the percentage so that the image they focused upon showed up more than 50 percent of the time. She even goes on to say that "A number of diverse researchers demonstrated that human intention can affect an enormous variety of living systems: bacteria, yeast, algae, lice, chicken, mice, gerbils, rats, cats and dogs." Research also included humans. McTaggart writes, "...intention has been shown to affect many biological processes within the receiver, including gross motor movements and those in the heart, the eye, the brain, and the respiratory system." So what are we tapping into here?

Well, obviously, there is more here than meets the eye. Not only are there larger forces at work, but these forces or energy fields are something that we can tap into to influence and help co-create our own reality. So does this mean that a little wishful thinking will help us win the lottery or manifest the man/woman of our dreams? Actually, there's a bit more to it than that.

210

First of all, the problem is that most of us are *not* focused. How many thoughts go through your head on any given day? How many of us multi-task and attempt to get a bunch of things done at once while really not accomplishing anything much at all because we're scattered? During the day, how many of us actually tune in to how we're really feeling, both emotionally and physically? In the Western world, we've become so busy that we just struggle from one day to the next. Very few of us were taught as children to be mindful about every task we do. Sure, when we were kids we might have had to focus to get our homework done, but we were probably listening to music at the same time so our minds were being pulled in a couple of different directions. Even as adults, how often do we really focus on the task at hand, especially if it is a simple one like brushing our teeth or washing the dishes? I don't know about you, but often my mind is thinking about what I need to get done that day. When we're in an unfocused state, it means that we're creating our lives "unconsciously" or "unintentionally".

So, what action steps do we need to take to use intention and to really tap into this powerful force? Here are four things that you can do to start using the power of intention in your life:

1. A good way to start is by being mindful. Mindfulness is something that has been in the news a lot more lately as research showing the health benefits of meditation continues to be done. Mindfulness refers to being focused on the present moment on whatever task you are doing. For example, if you are eating, you should be focused on the smells, tastes and textures of the food you are eating. In other words, you shouldn't be texting, checking your emails or watching TV while eating. Something else that is important to be mindful of is how we're feeling. Do you feel excited? Do you feel you have a deep sense of knowing you're on the right track or are you feeling anxious and stressed? Part of tapping into this force or energy field I talked about earlier is to be

211

mindful of how you're feeling because this can help guide you. What you focus on expands. Using intention to co-create your life involves tuning into this force that is a part of us but also greater than us. Some refer to this as the Universe or as God. Whatever you choose to name it is up to you.

2. The next step is to create some concrete goals or things you would like to accomplish. This could be something big like starting your own business or it could be around having a healthier lifestyle or it could be looking at a way to create your dream vacation. It doesn't matter what it is, just choose something that you would like to accomplish.

3. Thirdly, create doable action steps that will take you toward your goal. In their book, *The Success Principles: How to Get from Where You Are to Where You Want to Be*, Jack Canfield and Janet Switzer talk about "chunking it down".[4] What this means is that you look at your goal and write down all the steps that need to be taken to accomplish the goal. When you're doing each step, be mindful of what you are doing at the present moment. This will help you accomplish your tasks more quickly, efficiently, and enjoyably.

4. The fourth thing is focus. Focus is a key part of intention. Mindfulness is an aspect of focus but there are a couple of different levels to this. One is being mindful or focusing on the task at hand which I already mentioned. But, it is also important to focus on the end result, what you want to create or accomplish. I'm not talking about becoming obsessed. I'm talking about visualizing what you would like to create in your life and focusing on it in a relaxed manner. It's also important to realize that visualizing isn't enough. You also need to really *feel* what it would be like to have already achieved what you are wanting and focusing upon. While it may seem contradictory, using intention to manifest a goal also requires letting go and trusting that God/The Universe will provide what you need along the way.

Using the power of intention to co-create your life is a wonderful way to live life more fully and with greater awareness. This will not only influence your own life in positive ways, but also the world around you.

RESOURCES:

1. Dyer, Wayne. *The Power of Intention: Learning to Co-create Your World Your Way.* Carlsbad, California: Hay House Publishing, 2004. pp. 3-4.
2. The Institute of HeartMath. www.heartmath.org
3. McTaggart, Lynne. *The Intention Experiment: Using Your Thoughts to Change Your Life and the World.* New York: Free Press, 2007. p. xxii.
4. Canfield, Jack and Switzer, Janet. *The Success Principles: How to Get from Where You Are to Where You Want to Be.* New York: HarperCollins, 2005. p. 62.

Dr. Jennifer Harrison

CONCLUSION: PUTTING IT ALL TOGETHER

Sometimes it can seem overwhelming to make changes in our lives, even positive ones. We feel that we're already maxed out just trying to get through our day-to-day busyness. The key to overcoming stress is to make small changes and be consistent with implementing them daily. American author Mark Twain is quoted as saying, "The secret of getting ahead is getting started. The secret of getting started is breaking your complex, overwhelming tasks into small manageable tasks, and then starting on the first one." I wish you all the best and hope you will use the strategies I talked about in this book to help you Go From Your Stressed Self to Your Best Self™!

Dr. Jennifer Harrison

ABOUT THE AUTHOR

Dr. Jennifer Harrison holds a Bachelor of Science degree in psychology and zoology, is a Certified Athletic Therapist, Chiropractor, Certified BodyTalk Practitioner, educator, membership website creator, speaker and an award winning international bestselling author. She works with an amazing group of people at an interdisciplinary clinic in Calgary, Alberta, Canada. She also incorporates a wide variety of techniques into her practice. Dr. Harrison is currently the only person in the world with her training and experience.

Dr. Harrison has instructed at post-secondary institutions in Calgary. She taught Advanced Anatomy and Physiology for seven years at a local massage therapy college. She also did an annual guest lecture on the Role of Chiropractic in Sports Medicine at Mount Royal (College) University for the Athletic Therapy Program for seven years as well as a doing a guest lecture on mind body medicine at the University of Calgary. Dr. Harrison has developed professional courses for athletic therapists, massage therapists and physiotherapists and teaches across Canada.

In 2007, Dr. Harrison also became a BodyTalk Access Trainer. (BodyTalk Access is a one day course, available to anyone, in which you learn five core BodyTalk Techniques, including the Cortices Technique, which can be applied for daily self-care or to help family and friends.) In 2009, she was invited to join the International BodyTalk Association Access Review Committee which is responsible for evaluating applications from people around the world who want to study to become BodyTalk Access Trainers.

Dr. Harrison has a passion for writing. She has been featured in *Impact Magazine*, a Canadian health and fitness magazine, as well as the International BodyTalk Association newsletter, which reaches thousands of people around the world. She posts monthly articles on her membership website which cover topics on Bodymind Health, Nutrition, Exercise, Money and Abundance, Relationships and something she calls The Bigger Picture where she talks about the merging of science and spirituality. In addition to the release of her first book in 2015, *Stressed Self to Best Self™: A Body Mind Spirit Guide to Creating a Happier and Healthier You*, she also wrote an Editor's Choice Award winning chapter called "Overcoming Overwhelm" featured in New York Times bestselling author and Chicken Soup for the Soul co-creator Jack Canfield's book *The Soul of Success Volume One: The World's Leading Entrepreneurs and Professionals Reveal Their Strategies for Getting to the Heart of Health, Wealth and Success,* which became an international best-seller on launch day.

After studying the mind and body as separate entities at university, in the late 1980's she started studying mind-body medicine which demonstrates the interwoven, inseparable link between the mind and body. In 1990, she had a spiritual reawakening and embarked on a new path. Through her personal experiences as well as her studies, particularly with the BodyTalk System and through her church, she has developed a deep understanding of the mind-body-spirit connection and the impact stress can have upon it.

Dr. Harrison embraces the belief that we are all on a never-ending life journey, the purpose of which is to learn from both our "mistakes" and our successes so we can grow and help others. She also feels that to truly live up to our potential, we need to overcome the pressures of life. By implementing key strategies daily, you really can Go From Your Stressed Self To Your Best Self™!

You can connect with Dr. Jen via her web site:
http://drjenniferharrison.com/

Facebook: Dr. Jennifer Harrison

Twitter: @drharrison1

CPSIA information can be obtained
at www.ICGtesting.com
Printed in the USA
LVHW09s0315290918
591799LV00001BA/8/P